Unwrapping
the Inner Gifts of Christmas

Unwrapping
the Inner Gifts of Christmas

Tom Owen-Towle

Flaming Chalice
P R E S S

Flaming Chalice Press™
3303 Second Ave.
San Diego, CA 92103
Tel: (619) 933-1121
Website: www.tomo-t.com

10 9 8 7 6 5 4 3 2 1
First English Edition 2013

ISBN 13: 978-0-615-42748-5

Library of Congress Catalog Card Number: 2013952326

Cover and book design by CenterPointe Media
www.CenterPointeMedia.com

Dedication

To my beloved father, Harold Alexander Towle,
a work-weary man who came alive strumming
and singing every Christmas Eve with our
extended family, then died...as his fitting
farewell, on that very eve at the age of 81.

Contents

Introduction

"A lovely thing about Christmas is that it's
compulsory, like a thunderstorm,
and we all go through it together."
—GARRISON KEILLOR

Since my retirement from formal settled ministry, I've been combing my copious files, sermons, and assorted stuff related to 47 years of congregational leadership. Wouldn't you know it? I happened upon one of my earliest parish sermons (1968) entitled *Xmas Falls on December 25th This Year!* It was hand-written, on yellow-lined paper, and spawned my nascent pastoral convictions about Christmas:

> *Roughly 65 to 100 years after the Bethlehem birth four men told it as it was, for them then. Their distinct lessons remain wise commentary for us in 1968: Luke celebrated, Matthew anguished, John affirmed, and Mark was silent. What will it be for you, for me, this time around? Any of the above, some sort of combination, or our own peculiar account of the meaning of Christmas?*

I've revised this homily over the years, delivering it from various pulpits in countless Decembers. And I've included its most current iteration in the opening chapter of *UNWRAPPING the Inner Gifts of Christmas* as this book's launching pad. While my core message may have commenced some 45 plus years ago, it's taken me until now to harness its present configuration. Hence *UNWRAPPING* arrives as a set of unusual, sometimes edgy, essays—straightway from my heart to your hands.

But first, let's travel back to Christmas Eve, 2012.

As I'm prone to do, I was caroling amidst family and friends, belting out the Christmas ballads more heartily than usual, as a tuneful tribute to my father, Harold Alexander Towle, who had died 25 years before on Christmas Eve. Ever since Dad's death, on this most poignant day of the year, my soul has burst with scrambled feelings of profound joy and sadness. When Carolyn and I drove to the desert for our annual post-Christmas respite, this book was born. I wanted to compose a volume chiefly dedicated to my dad, which would pay tribute to the entire range of emotions we humans bear during this hardest holiday of the year.

Tell me if I'm mistaken: don't the Christmas holidays, when candidly addressed, teem with blues and gladness, delight and difficulty? Commercial traders like to bombard and seduce us with images of unsullied bliss; however that isn't the way the season typically plays out. In truth, there's plenty of joy to go around, but there's often depression saturating folk's bodies and hearts as well. Statistically, more despond exists in December than at any other time of the year. Bouts of SAD (Seasonal Affective Disorder) can assault even the healthiest among us.

Although the kernel of my evolving Christmas theology originated back in 1968, since my father's death in 1987 I've been paying closer attention to the multiple wisdoms inherent in the gospel accounts of

Jesus' birth. The fact that Matthew, Luke, Mark, and John conveyed distinct portrayals of this primal experience has made increasing sense to me. After all, their cumulative narratives epitomize the wholeness of the holiday season as you and I actually feel and face it.

Matthew, the initial gospel interpreter (at least, according to the order of our biblical records) communicated the pain and anguish of the birth. Luke, coming next, unleashed the familiar narrative of unbridled mirth. John, being the consummate philosopher, made a potent theological statement: "And the Word became flesh..." And, finally, Mark, the last of the storytellers, was conspicuously silent.

These four fundamental sentiments of sadness, joy, embodiment, and silence yearly constitute our basic emotional responses from Thanksgiving to New Year's Day. This sweeping range of reactions is what makes Christmas so complex, so relevant, so resourceful, and so utterly human. Moreover, these four outlooks and values are central to every season of life.

Peddling Christmas as merely a holly, jolly affair diminishes the fullness of our humanity as well as the scope of the original gospel narratives. Here's the key: when we bravely face, then embrace, the entire gamut of human emotions and experiences during December, we're spiritually prepared to do so the rest of the year. We become whole persons whenever we willingly confront the whole of life. And a good place to start becoming whole, make that holy, individuals is during the Christmas season.

Our family has long corresponded with a Hungarian minister who writes holiday notes, invariably concluding his epistles with the phrase: "Marry Christmas." At first, I considered correcting Sandor's flawed English but then thought better of it. Instead of just focusing upon merriment, Rev. Mathe unwittingly reminds us to *marry* all the different but crucial yin-yang elements of the holiday: happiness, sorrow, action, and quietude. To be sure, some years we will major in one sentiment or the other. At other times, we will bear all four...and more.

My Christmases are truly richer and more resourceful now than as a child or even as a young adult, because I've allowed myself to bathe in the whole spectrum of holiday experiences and emotions. In fact, I intentionally try to balance a combination of these sensibilities during Christmas—joy, sadness, service, and tranquility—rather than overdosing on one.

I think Garrison Keillor's on target. Whether we're Christians, Jews, Muslims or none of the above; agnostics, atheists, or theists; westerners or easterners; scrooges or shoppers; we can't avoid the swirl of the season. It's well-nigh impossible to make a mad dash from Thanksgiving to New Year's Day without being affected, and deeply so, by the seasonal eddy of mixed passions. Oh, I know, some folks retreat into veritable isolation during December, but few are consistently successful at hibernation. Why? Because one way or another, we're all touched, sometimes waylaid, or even transformed, by this singular time of the year.

Christmas is a compulsory course rather than an elective. Yes, it's like a thunderstorm (which is literally the case for those who live in wintry weather) that must be encountered. So, I say, let's go through Christmas together. Let's navigate it realistically and fully. There's more to Christmas than merely blissing out, descending into despair, or hiding from view. I'm pressing us to be *liberal* (broad-minded and bountiful) rather than *literal* (narrow-minded and rigid) in our responses to the Christmas happening. I'm goading us to unwrap the real and deeper gifts of Christmas. The mission of this book is to give us help and hope for the holidaze!

Charles Dickens penned: "God bless us, every one!"—a statement that may be faulty grammar but proves to be sound doctrine. It's an expression that Tiny Tim offers as a blessing during Christmas dinner at the beginning of *A Christmas Carol*, then is repeated at the end of the story to symbolize Scrooge's dramatic change of heart. For me, this blessing proclaims that the same God born in the baby Jesus signals an infinite and eternal Love that embraces every one—whatever your origin or orientation, class or conviction, gender or capacity, race or religion might be. Everyone (including folks missing on one's own personal guest list!) is emphatically welcome at the Christmas table.

Christmas is surely the time to endure a heartfelt sadness that won't go away; it's the time to relish nourishing and unexpected end-of-the-year whoopee; it's the time to hear and heed the persistent call to embody our better selves; and it's the time to marinate in serenity and hush. So let's wholeheartedly celebrate the birth of Jesus, but in its fullness not in some cookie-cutter, hackneyed, or puny fashion. Melancholy, introversion, elation, and kindness are equally honorable sentiments to feel, when genuinely and deeply felt.

A sidebar. Currently, there's an active and appropriate movement to pay sufficient homage to Hanukkah, Winter Solstice, Ramadan, and Kwanzaa as well as Christmas in order to be more inclusive of life's manifold traditions. I'm in agreement with this PC push, which I don't consider being *politically correct* so much as being *pluralistically conscious and personally compassionate*. Christ isn't the only reason for the season as many conventional Christians like to claim. There are multiple religious origins and rationales for sincere celebration during the days of December.

Nonetheless, Jesus, as sincerely understood and

hailed, remains the primary source of what motors the Christmas season. It's hard to contest that claim. So, I've decided to emphasize the birth of Jesus as the governing motif for UNWRAPPING. Other books have been composed about Hanukkah, Winter Solstice, Ramadan, and Kwanzaa, and I commend them to your mind and soul. After all, religious festivities shouldn't compete with, so much as complete, one another.

Moving ahead, let's address a couple of oft-missed ironies about Christmas. First, Jesus being a practicing Jew wouldn't have even celebrated his own birthday, since Jews thought birthdays were heathen events and not integral to their tradition. Whether or not Jesus broke free and commemorated his own birthday, we'll never know.

Second, no one really knows *when* Jesus was actually born. As my colleague Fredric John Muir astutely frames the issue:

> *With no clues to be found in the Gospel narratives, early church fathers of the third century placed his birth on May 20 and others on April 19 or 20. Clement, Bishop of Alexandria, nominated November 18. Hippolytus calculated that Christ must have been born on Wednesday, the same day God created the sun. Another church leader posited that the first day of creation coincided with the first day of Spring, on March 25,*

and contended that Jesus' birthday fell three days later, on March 28. All of these dates and any other ones are merely speculative best guesses.

Sometime, in the early years of the fourth century, Christianity had grown enough and felt secure enough to challenge all the other cultural and religious traditions. In one of the most astute moves ever, one that would characterize Christianity's growth until today, their leaders chose to appropriate popular ongoing holidays and piggyback on them.

Having no idea when Jesus was born, the early church selected the last day of Saturnalia as fitting for their observance. And that's the way December 25 was chosen.

Clearly, December 25th became both a calculated as well as a random date for the birth of Jesus. But what's the big deal anyway, since, as our 30th President Calvin Coolidge announced:

Christmas is not a time nor a season but a state of mind. To cherish peace and goodwill, to be plenteous in mercy, is to have the real spirit of Christmas.

UNWRAPPING the Inner Gifts of Christmas measures out a bowlful of spirited and spicy stories much like ladles of wassail—gleaned from my own 72-years-worth of Christmas lore as well as from the legends and recollections of other folks. These unprioritized reflections essentially fall under each of the four gospel perspectives on the birth of Jesus: grief, pleasure, benevolence, and serenity or some composite thereof. Of course, the gospel meanings often overlap and interlink. Suffice it to say, each of the ensuing essays is a trying or a testing, a short composition that attempts to analyze or interpret a given theme, and that theme is Christmas!

Of course, there's much more to be expounded about Christmas and its plentiful meanings; in fact, more's been written about Christmas than any other extant holiday. But this seems ample for one volume. I'll be satisfied if this book resembles what my magician buddies hope to claim about each of their effects: "It packs small but plays big!" UNWRAPPING is simply a modest-sized tome with curious, off-beat insights about Christmas: the holiday of holidays.

A couple more notes. Being an unapologetic holiday songster, I will regularly weave in passages from familiar carols to add some flavor to our swill. You'll recall that a carol was originally a song of joy accompanying a dance. Carols were initially frowned upon by the Church as not stately or somber enough for religious practice, but, by the 15th century, these lively tunes were fairly well-established in Western culture. Thank goodness! As for me and our household, songs were never sweeter or more rousing than those flowing from our tinsel-laden living room during Christmastide.

Our father, Harold Alexander Towle, was seldom one to rest. He was out selling insurance to clients, morning, noon, and in the evenings when we rarely ate dinner together as a family of four. He worked every day until he turned 81½, only a few months before he died.

Harold was a child of his times, a man destined to provide for and to take good care of his family, come rain or come shine. *But,* and this is a big but, every Christmas Eve, at our house, Dad would come home early from work and join our extended family for the holiday banquet. Circling the Christmas tree, along with Uncle Moschelle on the piano and Uncle Wilber on the saxophone, our work-weary father beamed, strumming the guitar or banjo and warbling Christmas carols with great gusto. My Dad's brother, Wilber, claimed, and rightly so that the only time he truly saw his kin full of joy was when Harold was singing. I'm still raised by the tender, piercing clarity of Dad's tenor voice.

So it's no surprise that Christmas was my favorite time of the year, since, among other pleasures, it was the sole/soul time we caught the best of our father's oft-suppressed ebullience. Christmas occasioned a fantasyland of delight and delicacies for this young boy, and continued to do so, pretty much up "until hark the Harold angel sing" died on Christmas Eve, 1987. Christmas has never been the same for me since that fateful night.

Yet strangely enough, while I've lost my Dad, I've grown in spiritual abundance. I sorely miss his honeyed timbre, his festive fervor, and his very presence, but I currently personify a more expansive version of what Christmas means and what Harold Alexander Towle represented at his fullest. Why do I say this? Because Dad knew ample pain and anguish, although he rarely revealed them. Harold also experienced the raw, often unnerving, power of silence and darkness and absence. And HAT, as he was nicknamed, was an unabashed embodier of service and mercy. As an Insurance Counselor (the title he chose), Towle gave unstintingly of his talents and time in attending to the well-being of others. I know that's one of the reasons I became a minister. Singing and serving, silent and sad…like father, like son.

So, here's the moral of *UNWRAPPING*. During Christmas time, I urge us to embrace all of its various and sundry emotions and experiences. Be willing to celebrate this season holistically rather than partially: soaking in sentimentality, facing sadness, being of service, and entering times of silence. Don't sell either yourself or the season short. For if you do Christmas well—that is, full-bore—you will most assuredly do the rest of the year full-bore too.

As they say, for every fat book, there's a thin book trying to get out. So, may this little book spur each of us to engage the nativity of Jesus as the catalyst for our own birthings and rebirthings...year after year after year. May Christmas in all of its assorted legends and multifaceted meanings inspire you and you and you and you and me to keep evolving and deepening into seasons beyond counting.

Think of it this way: you and I will never run out of Christmases until we run out of breath. So, let's start unwrapping the inner gifts of Christmas!

The Birth Stories

"To discover how to be truthful now, to be living now, to be loving now, to be human now is the reason we follow this star."
—W. H. Auden, *For the Time Being*

The four earliest recorded accounts of Jesus' birth are each different, thus illustrating the bedrock diversity of religious progressives who cherish variety, not conformity, in our spiritual ripening. So, let's revisit these discrete versions of the nativity scene and see what inner gifts we unwrap.

We start with Luke, because Luke captures the crux of what most folks customarily observe at Christmastime. Luke shared joy, the signature sentiment of the season. He answered the birth with a romantic narrative of visionary shepherds, unsophisticated wise guys, a paranoid, vindictive king, winged-messengers, and a virgin mother. A celebrative account flooded with the incredulous. Singing and dancing were unleashed throughout Bethlehem.

Luke posits that even reasonable people, when touched by the spirit, can do things divinely foolish. There's an exuberance to Luke's Christmas: the candles, the carols, the cookery, and the kindness. Luke describes the Nazarene's entrance with the lilt of poetry rather than the tedium of prose.

Luke reminds us to spend ample time during the holiday season mingling up close and personal with children. Accompanying little ones will certainly keep our adult world from being predictable and drab. Their companionship delivers a lilt to our voice and a lift to our step. In German the word for blessedness is *seelisch*, etymologically related to our word "silly"—

reminding sedate, solemn adults that in order to be blessed during the Christmas season, we must dare to become irrepressible practitioners of silliness, at least some of the time, therewith entering the realm of God, becoming not childish but childlike.

Luke would have resonated with the playfulness captured in the "The Twelve Days of Christmas." "On the first day of Christmas, my true love gave to me…a partridge in a pear tree…" This rollicking carol proceeds with a list of riotously inappropriate and ludicrous gifts, such as "two turtle doves, three French hens, six geese laying, seven swans singing, eight maids milking." On and on, the song gambols. Is it nonsense? To the mind, yes; to the heart, no! Not by a punchbowl of wassail. As my friend and colleague Rex Styzens invites: "Christmas is a risk to take. Shall we allow ourselves to be touched by sentiment?" I say yes, make that a resounding yes!

Then there's the Grinch! In Dr. Seuss's book, the Grinch couldn't steal Christmas. Even when he took the tree and the stockings and the turkey and all the gifts, the Grinch still heard every Who in Who-ville, the tall and small alike, singing on Christmas morning…even without presents! As Dr. Seuss tells it:

> And the Grinch, with his grinch-feet ice-cold in
> the snow, stood puzzling and puzzling: "How
> could it be so? Christmas came without ribbons!
> It came without tags! It came without packages,

boxes or bags!" And he puzzled three hours, till
his puzzler was sore. Then the Grinch thought of
something he hadn't before! "Maybe Christmas,"
he thought, "doesn't come from a store. Maybe
Christmas…perhaps…means a little bit more!"
And what happened then…? Well, in Who-ville
they say that the Grinch's small heart grew three
sizes that day.

Same with us. Our intellect may sort out fantasies from fact concerning Jesus' birth; it may even lure us into a fit of occasional scroogeness. But rationality can't steal or destroy the bone-deep joy intrinsic in the nativity scene. If we allow ourselves to feel the sparkle of Christmas, then our heart, just like the Grinch's, can't help but grow bigger!

Luke's vision was genuinely his own. While it's the one the western world knows and loves the best, it was only one.

Matthew carries some of the same Lucan narrative yet authors a definite variation, oft-forgotten amid our holiday revelry. Matthew registers pain when he responds to the barn birth. He alone of the early four gospel storytellers relates two incidents of anguish.

The first incident relates the agony that Joseph felt when he discovered that Mary is pregnant, not by him, and quietly considers a divorce. Joseph "was a man of principle and unwilling to put Mary to shame..." You and I realize that not every pregnancy is a planned or happy one. In fact, the statistics are staggeringly low, even among us moderns. Joseph is quite a shadowy character in the nativity drama. Scant news is reported about him. You have to wonder as you view the panoply of worldwide Madonna and Child portraits: "Where's Joseph? How come this man of solid character and faithfulness is missing when the Holy Family is depicted in art?" Joseph was a man of substance, "a just man" according to Matthew; despite all Joseph experienced, he remained committed to Mary, his betrothed, and to his son, Jesus. Joseph was an exemplary mate and father, if you ask me. His was a love that risked, sustained, and forgave without publicity or kudos.

And then there's the travesty laid bare in Herod's vicious plotting to murder Jesus and "all the male children in Bethlehem and in that entire region who were two years old and under." Herod failed to kill Jesus, but he didn't fail to slaughter the other blameless children.

Consequently, we mourn for all innocent people put to death because of brute power and greed. Right now, in this country and across the globe. A voice is heard in Ramah, wrote Jeremiah, sobbing and bitterly lamenting. It is Rachel weeping for her children because they are no more.

With unexpected pregnancy came anguish for Joseph. With the birth of Jesus came death to innocents.

You and I know full well that the holidays rarely deliver pure delight but are regularly awash in sorrow, even despondency. And it's vital to have this sentiment authenticated in the Holy Bible. So, if you come to the holiday season sad and out of sorts, this year or any other year, you should feel right at home. If you're alienated from a loved one, grieving over job turmoil or international strife, you're not alone. You're feeling feelings others have felt before you, still feel around you, and will feel long after you've died. I certainly resonate with the sentiment of Vietnamese Buddhist teacher, Thich Nhat Hanh, who regularly uses the expressions "joyful sorrow" and "sorrowful joy" to describe his journey through life. Isn't that the precise and paradoxical path we often traverse during the Christmas season?

There's a poignant story, retold by colleague Judith Walker-Riggs that begets tears of sorrowful joy during this darkening time of the year. Rev. Judith recalls the image of a most unusual crèche, where the little carved figures aren't painted, but made of different colors of wood. One of the wise men, for example, wears a gown in pale ivory that falls in curved folds around his brown feet. There's power and vitality and grace in the carving of each and every figure. The crèche is from Africa.

And more than that, the woods aren't mahogany

or rosewood, as you might think at a glance. For these figures are carved, you see, from thorns from the *egun* tree in Nigeria. They're big thorns, very wide at the base, but sharply narrowing, and they grow in the three colors used in the tableau. How strange yet fitting to carve something beautiful out of light and dark thorns, especially for a holiday that's the epitome of comfort and coziness. But carving the holidays from thorns, think of it; isn't that the way life often arrives, during this dank and stressful season? Perhaps your thorn is the death of a loved one, and this may be the first holiday without them. Or your thorn is someone having moved away. A severed relationship, a new illness diagnosed, a fatigued and worn-out soul: all these and countless other conditions can represent piercing thorns.

So we pilgrims of the spirit congregate in houses of worship as well as holy homes of hope, to create something beautiful and healing with our thorns. Alone, the task would prove daunting; but nestled in a beloved community, miracles happen, darkness delivers strange and wondrous gifts, the thorniest of thorns can be transformed. I know that to be true; I imagine you do as well.

Understandably, our personal losses—divorces, deaths, and disappointments—are magnified during this interval of presumed whoopee. When my father died in 1987, on Christmas Eve, I knew that my own holiday celebrations and memories would never be the same again. Indeed, no holiday season arrives now without my feeling the heart-rending combination of irrevocable joy and bone-deep sorrow. Unfailingly, I huddle close amid loved ones, sing lustily, and weep quietly during the grief-laden days of December. All the way to my grave, my Christmases will prove more painful yet more capacious in spiritual size.

The sadness of the holidays is neither superficial nor removable. Healthy people are deemed—to use a German word, *schemerzenreich*—rich in their ability to contain, not erase, sorrow. Sadness makes December a holy, as well as a *wholly*, season not just a gushy outburst of merriment.

Perhaps you've heard the story of the baptism of King Aengus by Saint Patrick in the middle of the fifth century. Sometime during the rite, Saint Patrick leaned on his sharp-pointed staff and inadvertently stabbed the king's foot. After the baptism was over, Patrick looked down at all the blood, realized what he'd done and begged the king's forgiveness. "Why'd you suffer this in silence?" the Saint wanted to know. The King replied, "Well, I just thought it was part of the ritual." As we welcome its sharp poignancy, sadness makes the season holy, not just a surge of superficial gaiety. Sadness is attached to the season; it's part of life's ritual.

So here's my hard-won counsel: don't smother

any of your sincere sorrow with pageantry, don't apologize for it, and for goodness sake, don't let Santa Claus or any therapist or pastor ever talk or buy you out of genuine sadness. Learning to befriend sorrow during the holidays may just prove to be one of the finest inner gifts we ever give ourselves.

Matthew's mission is to remind us that Christmas isn't merely for the jovial but also for those who are saddled with pain, maybe even more so. Christmas in its huge stretch of meanings, often ambivalent meanings, is a season of trouble and travail—yea, a season beset even by a possible divorce and actual deaths. So, if you're numbered among those who rarely find cause to be jolly at Christmas, then join the club, a hefty one at that. Indeed, if you resonate more with Matthew's response to Jesus birth than that of Luke, worry not...there'll always be room for you at the Christmas festival board.

And John. Alas, he leaves out any birth incident—pleasant or painful. He declares instead of narrates. Why? Probably because John's a theologian. His offering isn't a story but an affirmation, a claim, and a hope. "And the Word became flesh and dwelt (literally, *tabernacled* or *pitched tent*) in our midst," wrote John. A faith-claim that the same God that covenanted with Moses, argued with Gideon, struggled within Jeremiah...that same Spirit had returned, incarnating a fresh and robust love in the Bethlehem birth.

Oh, the many words, good and righteous words, we mouth in abundance during the holiday season, words that unfortunately seldom become flesh, remaining but pious platitudes. John reminds us to enflesh some of our noble moods this time around the calendar. As well as in the days and nights that follow. You know what? When we have ideas, they're often tame and wooden, but when ideas grasp us, then life occurs, they become flesh.

This season of the year, the Muslims are sometimes observing Ramadan, the lunar month in which the Qur'an was first revealed, a holy night in which the Word of God was born. And during December, Jews often complete their eight-day Festival of Lights (Hanukkah), commemorating the restoration of the temple in Jerusalem after the city was conquered and defiled.

Imagine what would happen if the followers of these three great Abrahamic faiths, along with anyone else who cared to join the caravan, would light lamps or candles as a consecration of the temple of peace in the very city that these great religions all claim. Imagine scrubbing the temple walls, not only in Jerusalem but also all over the world, to remove the bloody stains of secular and religious justification for warfare, genocide, bigotry, and slavery. Imagine that each of us might vow to pass the lamp of peace on to the next generation. Imagine that every one of us, who claims to be a card-carrying spiritual wayfarer, would speak peace, moreover, would incarnate peace…our very words become actual flesh, starting in our hearts and our homes. "Let there be peace on earth and let it begin with me…" resounds the song, first bellowed in the High Sierras of California by a choir of racially and religiously diverse youth, yearning for just such a dream to become a bit more true in their mid-1950's world. I know, because that's where I first learned this inspirational holiday ballad.

But there's more. Mark, actually the first gospel recorder of all, responds to Jesus' birth neither with joy nor with agony nor with affirmation but with silence. Amazingly, he reports absolutely nothing concerning the birth. Mark begins his gospel story with Jesus' baptism. The Christmas happening in all of its Lucan splendor, Matthean anguish, and Johannine proclamation is simply absent in Mark. It's impossible to know what drove Mark to silence upon learning of the birth of Jesus.

Let me give it a flailing shot; in short, some words about Mark's wordlessness. First, let's place Mark's response in the context of mythology. In our modern-day world, especially in the West, myth has generally stood as a synonym for falsehood. However, the Greek word *mythos* originally meant a truth that we humans feel or experience that can only be grasped in story or legend. Moreover, sometimes a powerful and compelling *mythos* dwells even beneath and beyond speech. It drives one to hush. Perhaps Mark was so impacted by the event of Jesus' birth that it became, for him, an ineffable reality. Mark must have felt the birth of Jesus, but, for whatever reason, he couldn't bring himself to write about it. We'll never know whether the gospeler Mark was unmoved or overwhelmed. In any case, he plainly didn't want to analyze or put it to words. Mark was rendered speechless.

Surely, Christmas is the season when we need to go quiet for a moment, many moments in fact, and just hunker down and fully listen. Christmas is the time to cease chattering, shopping, eating, even laughing or singing—long enough to embrace meaning beyond sound and replenishment without words. December is the season to be still and mute. Yes, silence will always constitute an honest and honorable response to the birth of the Prince of Peace. Luke celebrated, Matthew anguished, John affirmed, and Mark was silent.

In this strikingly dissimilar collection of scriptural responses to Jesus' birth lies the enduring message of the open-minded and large-hearted path. It summons each of us to compose our own versions of the Christmas story. We, like the four gospel writers, must meet and make our Christmas meanings, year after year after year after year...

Unwrappings

2 | Unwrapping

The Holiness of Waiting

"Serene, I fold my hands and wait,
Nor care for wind, nor tide, nor sea;
I rave no more 'gainst time or fate,
For lo! my own shall come to me."
—John Burroughs

I t's not only the hectic pace and the commercial overload of the season that unsettle us. On a deeper level, we humans are wracked with a basic inability to wait. We've got to have everything at once and for as long as possible. December becomes the season of racing and dashing rather than pausing and pondering.

A story from *Unplug the Christmas Machine*, a 1982 book by Jo Robinson, shows a mother finding her daughter crying in the closet on Christmas Day—just after she'd opened all the gifts she'd asked for. When the worried mother asked her daughter what was wrong, the girl answered, "If I had known this was all there was to Christmas, I wouldn't have worried so hard and waited so long."

To be sure, humans aren't constitutionally unable to wait. We're able to ease and inch up to the holidays: count days, keep secrets, slow down, soak in sounds and sights. We can wait. And I'm not just referring to children, because we adults ourselves are prime models of haste, as well, especially during the holidays. But we adults, the owners of the refrigerators and checkbooks, would be wise to show the way during Christmas time.

We can and must assist the little ones in learning the fine art of creative patience, of preparing their souls to enjoy life's precious moments. We might do well to tell our children, perhaps right after Thanksgiving...perhaps right after Halloween, nowadays: "Hey, dear ones: let's get our minds and bodies and hearts ready for Christmas. Let's slow down rather than rush this year. Okay? This is what I mean." Then demonstrate patience.

As the Advent season, literally the season of *waiting*, is launched, I would tender an old-fashioned case for the holiness—not just the necessity, but the holiness—of waiting imaginatively and compassionately.

For starters, let's remember that waiting isn't provisional time, the prelude to another moment yet to come; rather, waiting is time in itself. Waiting is valuable *per se*. Waiting gives us a chance to brood inventively. Waiting has its own grace and ingenuity. Here's a story that captures what I'm trying to say.

A trader docked his ship in an African port and hired the natives to carry goods inland on their backs for bartering with other indigenous people for their produce. Day after day, he got the people up early and walked them until late at night, always thinking of how much more profit he could exploit, if he could shorten the time that his boat stood empty in the harbor.

One morning he got up and found the transporters sitting quietly in a circle. The trader urged them to get up quickly and get started down the trail, but no one moved. After a long pause, the leader of the group announced, "We're going to sit still and wait until our souls catch up with our bodies!" The story ends with the Africans still sitting still. Sitting still during stretches of December, waiting for our souls to catch up with our bodies, is what I'm recommending.

Simply review your life. Aren't some of your earliest and fondest memories of waiting: kicking heels on the garden wall, anticipating one of your parents to come home from work on Friday afternoon, knowing you might be going out to dinner as a family? Waiting with other kids in line for the Saturday matinee movie? Waiting for the train to arrive, bringing your grandparents from out of town? Waiting around on the sandlot for the ballgame or dance recital to start?

Naturally, sometimes we were waiting nervously, but, in general, we've all experienced moments of waiting as a fun, cool, energizing time. Yet today, with instant gratification in our refrigerators, instant entertainment on our TVs and iPods, and instant transportation in our cars, we spend too little time in actual slow-motion expectancy, in preparing our hearts, in purely waiting.

Waiting can prove to be a gift, not a curse–a gift of time. Time to waste: to waste in the discovery of a world, and the people in it, in all their weird and wonderful variety. Remember "it's the time you've wasted on your rose," wrote Antoine St. Exupery in *The Little Prince*, "that makes it so important." Oh yes, it's the time you waste on yourself in meandering around the neighborhood on an extra slow walk. It's the time you waste humming alone. It's the time you waste leisurely perusing a book or soaking in a bath-tub. It's the time you waste on your partner, giving a lingering back rub. It's the time you waste playing cards as a family. It's the time you waste kicking at pebbles, watching the stars and the birds, noticing all the quiet–unimportant yet essential–things that hap-pen every day around you.

One of my prime time-wasters is reviewing and repeating, over and over again, the basic moves of a magic trick. Being the inveterate multi-tasker I am, I can manipulate effects while I'm watching the news or listening to a beautiful piece of music.

It's the time you "waste" serving food at the home-less shelter; it's the time you "waste" on neighborhood kids playing in the park; it's the time you "waste" paying an unexpected visit to an infirm member of your community; and it's even the time you "waste" engaging a stranger at the store. In wasting such time, we surprisingly often uncover vital meanings of our lives.

And during the holidays, it could be the time you waste weaving a scarf, sculpting a candle, or writing a heartfelt note on a holiday card to a friend. It might be the time you spend curled up relaxing, on your knees praying, or on your feet singing to some person whose holidays might be less, even lost, without a stirring batch of carols. All these things, and more, can furnish your life with leisurely, slow-down rituals in unhurried preparation for the coming of the Festival of Lights.

Waiting is so hard for us modern-day sprinters, but wait we must. For we owe ourselves, more than any other gift, a nourished soul. Did you know that a person arriving at a traditional Japanese monastery is turned away at first? It always takes three days to get in. So during that time of waiting, visitors are forced to sit alone in the woods or take a languorous walk in the snow. And what happens? While waiting, often insights appear; even an inner birth might occur.

That's the point: we wait during this season so that more *inner* events can unfold in the midst of all the *outer* hoopla. Our interiors can be fed in the pregnant stillness of waiting. For the true gifts of the holidays don't exist *out* there but *in* here, if we but wait patiently and allow them to be born.

So I ask: during December, what do you need to wait upon and who might you be waiting for? Can you take some time, sufficient time, to muse keenly, sing softly, just breathe in and breathe out in a peaceful corner of your home? Can you just sit tranquilly as Mary did awaiting the birth of her baby Jesus?

I know we hanker to get up and go, wanting to seize the day. Yet the Holy Scriptures, in every land and every era, admonish us to wait. "Could you not watch with me one hour?" Jesus rebuked his industrious, antsy disciples.

So much of that first Christmas was spent in waiting. Those two opening chapters of Luke's gospel—two of the longest chapters of the entire bible—are full of people waiting: Elizabeth and Zechariah, Mary and Joseph, the shepherds of Bethlehem, Simeon and Anna, just waiting and then waiting some more, for enduring peace to be born.

Sincere, bold spiritual pilgrims know well that we never ultimately arrive on our journeys; rather, we're ever waiting and searching, searching and waiting for new truth and growth, fresh joy and challenge to come our way. We can never grasp either the fullness of the Great Spirit or the fullness of any great holiday, but we can experience glimpses of the sacred in the unlikeliest of haunts, if we but wait expectantly, mull calmly, and probe deeply.

Therefore, let us watch and wait, center in and center down, pray and breathe and sing. And along with deep breathing, I recommend hearty singing. In England, at this time of year, children go from door to door singing: these young carolers are called "waits." While we're waiting, we too can sing.

And while waiting, let's be *perceptive*. Instead of eliminating our routines, we can illuminate some of them. See what can be, not simply what has been. Look beneath the surface, beyond the literal, and behind the ruts of the season.

Let's be *conceptive*. Generate a new custom or commitment, utterly outside the boxes of your past. And conception means a shared enterprise, so collaborate, give birth alongside someone else to something unspeakably newfangled and beautiful.

Finally, while waiting, be *receptive*. Be expectant; open your spirit to those gifts that might just emerge from waiting more patiently than ever before.

Down deep in the marrow of our souls, we know that ours is still a waiting world, and that you and I must become eternal waiters. For no matter what verities we attain, love we perform, excellence we achieve, we'll end our lives somewhere in the middle, as partial beings–waiting, waiting, waiting...

The Treasures of Darkness

"I will give you the treasures of darkness
and the hoards in secret places."
—Isaiah 45:3

"All the outward show of the season is a vain attempt to create Christmas, to control it, to make it come. It will come, I have learned. But it comes in spite of, not because of, our efforts. It comes not in the outward show but rather in the inner darkness. The wise men could only see the star because of the darkness. It was a lonely cave beside the inn that was filled by the birth of love. The shepherds who waited on a lonely, dark hillside and trembled in fear were the first to hear the news."
—Rev. Earl Holt

Before we know it, Winter Solstice, the shortest day and longest night of the year, will be upon us. Remember in pre-Christian times, the Norsemen lit yule logs to drive back the engulfing winter's darkness. Plus Hanukkah and Christmas, both festivals of intense luminosity, lie just around the corner.

Given the convergence of these three holy seasons, you'd normally be reading an essay on the wonders of light, right? Instead, I want to throw something off-speed. Not a nasty pitch, but a tantalizing curveball that every one of us is capable of hitting.

Here's my pitch: only when we dare to welcome, then embrace, the blessings of darkness, will we become grown-up religious travelers. My whole approach to the Christmas season certainly has been deepened, actually altered, by the reflections of the progressive theologian Matthew Fox, who advocated in his watershed book *Original Blessing* (1983) that the Western World was long overdue to come to creative grips with the blessings of "endarkenment" rather than always gravitating, especially during the days of December, to a philosophy of "enlightenment." His challenge to "befriend darkness" was starkly perceptive.

You may be familiar with the ancient tale of the inebriated man on his hands and knees underneath a street lamp searching the sidewalk. A friend comes by and says, "Ralph, what in the world are you doing out here on your hands and knees?" "Well, I'm hunting for my house key," Ralph replied. "I lost my house key." The friend got down on his hands and knees too. "Show me where you lost it, and I'll help you," he said. "Oh, I lost it way over there in the grass," Ralph said. "Then, why in the world are you looking for it out here on the sidewalk?" the friend asked. "Well, because this is where the light is!"

I've a strong feeling that a lot of us come to worship services, particularly during the holiday season, because somehow, somewhere we've lost something. Maybe we're not even sure what we lost or where we lost it, but we're convinced that a religious community might just be where the light is. After all, it's been proven that there are three main reasons why people pursue a religious abode: hurt, home, and hope...in short, in seeking a good congregational fit, folks are invariably negotiating some sort of hurt and desire a home of hope—reasonable, not fanciful, hope.

A temple or church or mosque or sangha *should* be a sacred place and people where there is light; stick around it for a while, and you'll invariably find lots of illumination. But an open-minded, life-affirming religion challenges us to experience *both* the blessings of endarkenment *and* the riches of enlightenment. However, during the December holidays, let's face it, we tend to rush to light candles, even growing addicted to the blaze of tinsel and ornaments. We're prone to an easy, quick conversion of this darkening time of the year into harried rituals and compulsive partying. Alas, we're disposed to smother anything dark in a blaze of light.

Yet we pay a price for our light-binge. We grow lopsided whenever we embrace light and banish darkness—when, in truth, both realities can deliver wisdom and meaning. Human existence is incorrigibly water and soil, noise and quiet, masculine and feminine, sorrow and joy, light and dark, and our task as humans is to explore the entire range of the continuum, rather than gravitate to one snug, convenient, comfortable corner of reality. As my tennis buddy puts it: "Tom, there's a yin and yang to every *thang!*"

In more formal religious language, as Matthew

Fox goes on to remind us, the Hebrew Scriptures declare: "And there was evening and there was morning, one day." You see, each 24-hour sweep is unified, of a whole. Light and dark, day and night are merely different seasons, comprising the entire mysterious reality we designate as life. Therefore, a light-dominated spirituality is superficial, thin, and incomplete; it lacks the deep, dark roots that nourish and ground the whole life-journey. The truth is, we'll never quite mature spiritually, if we always conduct our lives with the lights on.

The treasures of the dark are many. Dreams emerge in the dark. Our earth came into being when darkness brooded upon the face of the deep. Indeed, *humus*, from which our germinal concepts of humor, humanness, human, and humility all sprout, refers to the dark, organic portion of soil. We evolve from the darkness of our mother's wombs. Never forget: in mystery we're born, in mystery we live, and in mystery we die. All mystery is about the unknown, the silent, the dark. And what about stars: those natural, luminous, celestial wonders that filled the sky when Jesus was born and continue to do so every day and night of reality?

As Solstice approaches every winter, I implore you to seize some time, daily, a few minutes will suffice (no need to compete with either yogis or monks), and sit in the dark—alone, quiet, and still—consciously blessing all that grows in the dark.

For the December dark, dank, and cold—even in sunshiny Southern California—harbingers a time for productive spiritual brooding. In the midst of all the holiday hysteria, when everyone's romping around in a commercialized frenzy, winter reminds us to slow down, turn around, focus inward and weigh what truly matters in our lives. Come to your senses. Find your mind. Visit your soul.

Winter is traditionally thought of as a low-energy period, a time even of despondency. Yet this dark season of the year, when we don't run from it but rather surrender to it, can be a rare time of internal renewal and deepening. Have you noticed: in winter time, we can better hear the pounding of our very hearts, for there's more silence all around?

So, I urge you to pay your interior castle a long-overdue visit, travel toward the primal, the instinctive, and the earthy. Down, down, down, back, back, back...use this season to connect with your core, your essence, your dark, deeper being.

Remember that the dark season of the year is a time of hibernation for both the plant and the animal world. It should also be a quiet time, an inward time, a time of gathering energy and strength for human beings as well. We humans also grow, most profoundly, when we affirm the shadow side of our character, meet head on our inner demons, and endure the inexplicable, dark sorrows that befall us.

So, I ask you: what is it that you need to brood about or wrestle with in the silence and darkness of your solitary soul? Whatever it may be, I summon you to travel beneath the cheap glare of the season and dive deeply into your darkness…and emerge as a more expansive person. Probe beneath the pervasive blaze of the season and descend into the quietude of your being.

Brood about the brokenness in your life and that of the larger world. Brood about what you plan to do with your remaining years on this planet, starting here and starting now. Brood not to despair, rather brood to cleanse and ground your being…readying your heart for a soulful, embodied response.

Furthermore, it seems to me to be a wise season to recall the importance of helping our own offspring as well as the children of the greater world to better acclimate themselves to life's insistent darkness. From the moment children leave the womb and enter daylight, they experience an abundance of fears born of imagination and reality. We older, more experienced life-travelers need to help the younger ones confront their fears rather than be overwhelmed by them. Often in a well-intentioned yet futile effort to rid children of natural anxiety, nervous adults flood their lives with artificial, overpowering light, when we'd do better to assist them in finding their way amidst the physical and moral dark that will accompany them all their days and nights.

The darkness need not destroy anyone, young or old. In fact, it won't. Just as Moses saw Yahweh in the light and lived, so we can face the mysterious, scary, healing darkness and live. There's a poignant observation by the Spanish philosopher Miguel Unamuno who pondered Goethe's dying words about "Light, more light." Unamuno responded by saying, "No, not more light, but more warmth. We die of cold not of darkness. It's the frost that kills and not the night."

Nevertheless, let's be honest, sometimes life's emptiness seems overwhelming, and we get lost in it. Whether in our own family or in the larger community, there exist countless hurting people who could use some CPR (a "compassionate, personal response"), who could benefit from someone willing to listen to, even shoulder for a spell, some of their despond.

So I invite you to find ways during the holidays to companion folks struggling in emotional and financial darkness: to help them not just with money or canned goods, both of which are necessary, but be willing to serve the lost and least up close. Don't just exchange clothes, exchange some power. Dare to touch those who are seldom touched; dare to make visible those who are perennially invisible to human sight and care. Homelessness is real, so is depression, so is death, and all three pervade our culture during the damp, dreary days of December. The seasonal darkness is often magnified, and the best we humans can do is bunch close, hold one another, and, when blessed, be lovingly carried to the other side.

A few years ago, our beloved sister-in-law, Mary Sue Manley died suddenly of a brain aneurysm, at the age of 60. It was in mid-December, just as we were readying ourselves for the manifold delights of the holidays (Sue particularly was a guiding spirit in the celebrations of our clan). Shocked, we surrounded her hospital bed, where she lay unconscious. We wept and prayed, gnashed our teeth and soothed her brow, shook our souls in dismay while paying homage to her extraordinarily positive life. There was seldom a more consistently, upbeat human being than Mary Sue Manley: sister, partner, step-mother, aunt, grand-mother, colleague, and friend.

She simply epitomized our faith at its finest: for Sue knew in the marrow of her soul that we belonged to a Love that will never let us *go*, will never let us *down*, and will never let us *off*, to use the phrasing of colleague Rob Hardies, and she tried to embody such love, day in and day out.

So, it wasn't out of character that late the very afternoon of Sue's death, most of our family, children included, left the hospital to attend Dr. Seuss's production *How The Grinch Stole Christmas*. Sue had been instrumental in coordinating this specific excursion;

clearly, she would have wanted us to go, indeed we felt her palpable presence throughout the play.

In a profound and mystical way, the fulsome beauty of both darkness and light were married that afternoon as we mourned and reveled in this enchanting musical together.

They continue to yearn to marry every day and night of our pilgrimage.

Keeping All These Things

"May we not 'spend' Christmas or 'observe'
Christmas, but rather 'keep it.'"
—PETER MARSHALL

"And when the shepherds found Mary and Joseph, and the babe lying in a manger, they made known the saying which had been told them concerning this child; and all who heard it wondered at what the shepherds told them. But Mary kept all these things, pondering them in her heart."
—Luke 2: 17-19

A midst the joyous proclamation and amazement of this season, Mary's radical introspection appears anomalous. Christmas seems the season to be bold and public, festive and auspicious, hardly the time to withdraw and ponder matters. But wait a minute; in fact, pause several moments.

Here's my counsel, Mary's counsel. During each December day that lies ahead, steal (yes, steal because other folks aren't programed during the holidays to hand over hunks of peacefulness to you!) some quiet time away by yourself. Find a corner within your house and within your heart to be still and silent, in order to muse upon life's ordinary marvels and soak in the everyday sensations that make your very existence an unspeakable blessing. Ponder the enduring resources beneath the ephemeral enticements. Eternal beauty and joy dwell within your grasp, if your soul stands wide-open. Therein will your December days become holy rather than hectic.

Mary's response to Jesus' birth is precisely what

most of us frenzied holiday celebrants covet, yet unless we take that is "seize," time to ourselves during December, we will be thoroughly tinseled out by the time the New Year lands.

Keeping means something else as well. To *keep* is to hold onto what we believe to be precious. It means preserving rather than just observing. Mary was concerned about storing a spirit that would survive beyond the birthday bash. She knew that lots of people could commemorate for a spell, but that a religious few would doggedly struggle to keep joy and justice, peace and hope flourishing for any extended, lonely haul...long after the hoopla dies down.

As poet E. E. Cummings penned: "love is the every only god...who spoke this earth so glad and big." May our holiday spirit grow "glad and big," touching everyone and everything we encounter along life's path strewn with marvels.

Coping with the Holidaze

"To perceive Christmas through its wrappings
becomes more difficult with every year."
—E. B. White

I n the language of China, the word *crisis* is made up of two characters. Each character comprises half a word, the first referring to *danger* and the second to *opportunity*. Hence a crisis is literally a "dangerous opportunity."

Periodically, over the sweep of my 47-year ministry, I've led or participated in *Coping with Christmas* workshops. They've also been named: *Getting through the Holidays Happily and Healthfully* or *Welcome to Holidays Anonymous*.

I often launch the series in mid-October, giving everyone a running start, tackling all the various and sundry seasonal festivals from Halloween through New Year's Day. These workshops enable folks to band together, swap our respective anxieties, then exchange ways not merely to survive but also to welcome the holidays, whenever possible or desirable. Here are some evocative notes from these workshops.

With respect to *Halloween*, I suggest two exercises: first, list what or who is truly "hallowed" or precious in your current life; second, name the things that scare you and describe how you can face (not erase) said demons.

With respect to *Thanksgiving*, name three realities and relationships for which you are genuinely grateful, starting with yourself and spreading outward. Also, describe two sources of true ingratitude, since as Martin Luther King, Jr. reminds: "creative maladjustment or discontent" often leads to personal growth and societal change.

In anticipating both *Hanukkah* and *Kwanzaa*, both festivals of liberation, enumerate the physical, vocational, and spiritual bonds that presently enslave you. Address what it will take to bring you greater freedom and lasting release from these slaveries.

As for *Advent*, what are you brooding about *and* what are you waiting for this particular December? Be specific in responding to both queries. With respect to *Winter Solstice*, how are you dealing with the increasing darkness and quietude of the wintry days and nights? Do you have a need for more light, enlightenment, lightness in your life? If so, why, and how do you plan to obtain it?

Thinking of *Christmas*, what hankers to be born in your life this year? And as you face the *New Year*, rather than making a list of improbable resolutions, describe one or two bold initiatives that will likely keep you awake and vital in the coming year.

In doing these workshops I've also compiled a list of 35+ words and phrases such as customs, caroling, anger, cold, death, Jesus, money, masks, disappointment, eating, mistletoe, boredom, goodwill, blizzards, children, menorah, snow sports, death, wonder, service, stockings, fireplace, guilt, joy, giving, receiving, relatives, peacefulness, Santa Claus, shopping, darkness, holiday cards, arguments, love, loneliness, and hope. I invite workshop participants to write their emotional responses to each of these words in light of holiday seasons past and present. They are encouraged to add other words of their own to evoke additional memories. The conversations are often both wrenching and reassuring.

Additionally, workshoppers swap notes on how to protect ourselves when we're feeling raw and vulnerable during the holidays. We swap proven tips on avoiding situations that perennially stress or upset us. We encourage tactics to curtail outside commitments and nurture periods of inner peace. We share clear-cut ways to say: "Not now, but perhaps later"… or "No, but here's a compromise," or "No, no, no." We exchange ideas on innovative and beneficial ways to celebrate the holidays, planning activities that are enjoyable and meaningful rather than burdensome, trite, or stale. We journal to create inner strength while exploring unresolved feelings or wounds from the holidaze—all in all, clarifying how we can better take care of ourselves during December.

Holiday Habits

"Christmas . . . is not an external event at all,
but a piece of one's home that one
carries in one's heart."
—FREYA STARK

H ere's a letter I wrote my wife, early on in our marriage, the second one for both of us. After 40 years, we're still grinding away at making our "holiday habits" more palatable and pleasurable.

Dearest Carolyn,

The holidays can be hellish at best but especially full of snags for couples, claim the experts. Why? Because each partner brings different histories to and hopes for the holidays, be they birthdays, Valentine's Day, three-day weekend festivities, anniversaries, or Thanksgiving.

Christmas is the most conflicted of all holidays, especially for partners and families. Each of us, Carolyn, has practiced certain customs in our upbringing as well as in our first marriages. I remember our initial Christmas together. It was downright awkward, even painful, because neither of us would compromise our holiday habits, some of which were diametrically opposed. We wrangled over tree size, kinds of decorations, type, range, and cost of gift-giving and much more. When your kids, my stepchildren, understandably sided with you, I was an ornery puss, the odd guy out.

In recent years, when we've allowed the other partner to do what he or she enjoys most during the Christmas season, without cajoling or blaming, we've been a markedly happier tribe. We've learned that there's plenty of room and time from Halloween to New Year's Day for each of us to remember and revel in self-styled fashion.

Last year I tried a new holiday gifting pattern that was a roaring success for both of us. It was like we'd struck gold, at least for the moment. However, before we jump to cheery conclusions, let's see how this custom wears. Instead of giving you one huge and gorgeous gift on December 25th, I surprised you with a series of modest yet meaningful notions, both material and spiritual, usually quite playful, every day from December 13th on. The string ran out around December 27th, because my imagination had been stretched to its limit.

My gifts were cool to plot and present: an unexpected trip to the movie, *A Christmas Story*; the polishing of your wedding ring as well as mine; new floor mats in your car; scissors that actually cut, hidden in your dresser drawer; a cooperative rather than scroogish attitude toward the buying of "O Tannenbaum" (it was neither gigantic nor paltry, rather mid-sized); a 29 cent package of tree ornament hooks for next year; an evening of sensual poetry read while caressing your sleepy head; a poinsettia deluxe that lasted until Easter; a book of coupons to get your car washed...

This continual christmasing worked not only for December but has given me fresh and quirky ideas for startling you a bit in the New Year.

All my love,
Tom

I'm Tired of All the Holiday
Handwringers!

"My idea of Christmas, whether old-fashioned
or modern, is very simple: loving others.
Come to think of it, why do we have to
wait for Christmas to do that?"
—Bob Hope

I'm tired of all the holiday handwringers! So here's some preventive medicine for combating the seasonal blues...mine and yours and theirs. As my friend puts it: "There are 10 solid rules for beating the holiday blues: first, go out and do something for somebody. Then repeat the good deed nine times, either with the same person or with somebody new each time."

Some other specific suggestions:

- Celebrate the entire *Twelve Days of Christmas* rather than only the 25th. It's more pleasurable and puts you in giving-shape for the rest of the 365. Our family has grown fairly adept at bestowing modest, ingenious gifts all during December: things such as swap meet surprises; unexpected favors; and hugs away from the mistletoe. You get the idea.

- Remember that the best, most durable playthings your children will ever get are you. For them, actually for all creatures near and far, Love is best spelled T-I-M-E. As Derrick Jensen bluntly puts it: "What your children really want for Christmas is your love, but if they can't get that, they'll settle for a bunch of electronic crap!" So give your little ones a parent for Christmas, without any price tag attached. Then stay in practice.

- Be ecologically sensitive. Make some treasures from trash. Rejoice as you recycle. Second-hand items and "twice-loved" toys often prove to be memorable favorites.

- Flabbergast, or at least, astound somebody. Plant flowers in your friend's garden. Send warm notes to people who'd least expect them from you. Give a contribution or membership in someone's name to a cause of their choice. These are more than random acts of kindness: they're neither arbitrary nor purposeless; they're planned.

- Children are innately creative and generous souls if steered in the proper direction. Help them make gifts to give, and they may momentarily forget lusting after their own gifts.

- Remember shut-ins, prisoners, orphans, the ill, anyone who lives with minimal support or on the margins. Plan caroling or outings to rouse them from their doldrums. Then continue such visits after the holidays. As writer Shirley Chisholm reminds: "Service is the rent you pay for room on this earth."

- Organize a toy swap in your neighborhood on December 21. The exchange can be preceded by telling the dramatic story of the Winter Solstice and followed by convivial drink and merriment.

- Teach someone how to play a musical instrument, to bake a pie, to perform a magic trick, or to knit something. Think of other skills you might share in the days ahead. You're just getting warmed up. You possess unique skills and gifts that only you are able to share. Then invite your companion to impart something to you.

- Shed two of your precious (non-rummage stuff) adult belongings: giving one to a family member and the other to a person who might actually need it.

Here's an example of giving that worked for me this past Christmas Eve. During the rainy morning, I went to our Uptown Faith Community Center to hand out gloves, ponchos, and food to our homeless sisters and brothers. So many personally thanked us for being present on this day rather than shopping or simply closing down the Center. When one man said:
"I can't imagine your being here on Christmas Eve," I replied, "Not to argue with you, my brother, but I can't imagine myself not being here, being anywhere else. This is precisely where I want and need to be. We're placed on earth to

serve and be served by one another. I reckon com-passion to be the main message of Christmas!"

Finally, receiving is as spiritual an art as giving, and December is one season to stay in shape. So, be on tenterhooks, stay in a reachable mood, have your arms open and antennae tuned. Don't shut down your heart; don't close up your spirit. Remember we come into life, as babies, with our fists closed. We die with our hands wide-open. The interval between birth and death is meant to be spent in increasingly opening our hands both in giving and receiving. And we can do neither if our fists remain closed.

May Our Own Words Become Flesh!

"I have always thought of Christmas as a good time; a kind, forgiving, generous, pleasant time; a time when men and women seem to open their hearts freely, and so I say, God bless Christmas!"
—CHARLES DICKENS

Let's peruse the stable of holiday carols for examples that salute the Johannine proclamation that "The Word became flesh..." encouraging us to go and do likewise. It's tempting to bypass altogether the hefty social witness inherent in the Christmas songs. Yet we slide (or should I say, sled) by the prophetic bite of the carols at great cost to our spiritual maturation. Here are but a few useful illustrations.

Good King Wenceslas recounts the compassionate deeds of Wenceslas, the holy ruler of 10th century Bohemia. Wenceslas was especially known for his abundant munificence at the Feast of St. Stephen, held on December 26th. "Therefore, Christian folks, be sure, wealth or rank possessing, ye who now will bless the poor, shall yourselves find blessing." In sum, in blessing the hurting of humanity, you are truly blessing yourself.

Oh Holy Night has a verse, within its otherwise Christocentric story of salvation that urges singers to heed the humanitarian example of Jesus to become carriers of justice and peace during our holiday lives and beyond: "Truly he taught us to love one another, his law is love, and his gospel is peace; chains shall he break, for the slave is our neighbor, and in his name shall all oppression cease." You can't find anywhere in the treasure-trove of holiday music a more compelling depiction of Jesus as a shameless social activist!

From the English 12th century carol entitled *The Friendly Beasts* (also affectionately known as the *Song of the Ass*) even the animals get into the act of servant-hood: the donkey carries Jesus's mother; the cow delivers a manger; the sheep brings wool for Jesus' blanket; and the dove coos the baby Jesus to sleep. "Thus every beast by some good spell in the stable dark was glad to tell, of the gift he gave Emmanuel, the gift he gave Emmanuel." When all is said and done, all living beings are invited to celebrate and support the Bethlehem babe.

My college roommate, who went on to become an eminent biblical scholar, relates his 7-year-old-son's earnest Christmas day prayer: "God, please teach me how to be a *helper!*" Or in words I often offer our eight grandchildren:

"Grandma and I have only one wish for each of you in the years ahead; may your lives be good gifts to the world!"

And here are two modest, modern day accounts of young people enfleshing their noble words, of standing up for what is loving and good, "being good for goodness sake" as the carol prompts. Not being good because we're going to get paid or be recognized, but being good because that's the reason we're alive. "Being good for goodness sake" goes directly to the heart of the compassionate life, doesn't it?

The first incident of goodness recalls a young girl in our local youth group who was hardly counted among the popular girls. Melanie wasn't deemed either pretty enough or socially adept. Nonetheless, every December, she would go from house to house in her neighborhood, visiting shut-ins, even knocking on the doors of people Melanie didn't know. Of course, this was an era when such behavior was absolutely safe.

When folks would come to their front door, Melanie would say something like: "I live in the neighborhood, and I just wanted to see how you're doing and check if there was any chore you might need done during these twelve days of Christmas. I'm here to serve you, if you need me." She also brought home-baked cookies along with her. And if no one came to the door, Melanie would inconspicuously leave the cookies on the porch with a guileless "Merry Christmas and Happy New Year" note attached.

She even *thanked* the neighbors, whether or not they gave her something to do. Melanie was amazing and still stands out in my life as someone whose words genuinely became flesh during the holidaze.

Did Melanie do this out of caring for her "neighbors"? Of course. Did she perform these acts of goodness to make herself feel better? You bet she did. If the basic descriptor of Jesus' birth was Emmanuel which literally means "God with us," then Melanie

condensed Christmas into those very three words—
"God with us"—and aspired to follow suit by "being
with others."

And here's a second story of a young person
who also experienced John's response to the birth of
Jesus. Our congregational member told the story of
her young son serving and sharing a meal with the
homeless, during our interfaith winter shelter stint,
years back:

> As we cooks worked in the kitchen, my son Aar-
> on wandered around the tables in the Common
> Room, a little bored until he spied a deck of cards.
> And in the open and bold manner of a nine-year
> old, he looked up and asked the guests, "Does
> anybody here know how to play poker?" Chuck-
> ling, a group formed, playing and arguing about
> my son's arbitrary rule-making.
>
> When supper was ready, Aaron came over to me
> with a puzzled look and asked quietly, "Mom,
> aren't we going to wait for the homeless people?"
> And I responded, "Honey, these are the homeless
> people." Then he said, in a hushed voice: "But,
> Mom, they look just like everybody else!"
>
> And I knew then I had given my son a gift more
> precious than anything I'd ever put under the
> Christmas tree. Many weeks later, on rare rainy

nights here in San Diego, we wondered aloud if some of his poker partners had a dry place to sleep. Now, you see, for us homelessness is no longer a social problem; it has names and faces of my son Aaron's poker partners.

No Room at the Inn

"And Mary gave birth to her first-born son and
wrapped him in swaddling clothes and laid him
in a manger, because there was no place
for them in the inn."
—Luke 2: 7

We tend to sentimentalize as well as sanitize the barn birth. The delivery of Jesus may have been "immaculate," depending upon your personal theology, but the actual circumstances of the nativity were anything but spick-and-span. The unmistakable fact is that a manger is a trough for feeding animals. It's filled with mud and dirty straw. Manger derives from the same root as "mangy," meaning squalid, infested with the disease of parasites in pigs and cows.

In order to counter the repulsiveness of the setting, we're prone to fabricate playful pageant dialogues such as the one our parish children once conveyed: When Joseph and Mary came to the door of the inn, the boyish innkeeper bravely carried through his assigned line, with a slight addition. Responding to their request for room, he said: "I'm sorry, there isn't room in the inn, but wouldn't you like to come in for a cup of coffee or a beer?"

Here's an alternative approach. A while ago, a group calling itself the *Committee for Creative Nonviolence* submitted a drawing for a sculpture to be part of the Annual Christmas Pageant of Peace in Washington, D.C. The sculpture depicted a homeless family—father, mother, and baby—all standing on a heating grate in the middle of a snow-covered city. The caption below read: "Still no room at the inn!"

The Court ruled that the sculpture could not be

placed in the pageant, because it didn't incorporate the "true and traditional" symbols of Christmas such as Santa Claus, reindeer, mistletoe, fir trees, and the like. How ironic! Isn't the Christmas story basically about a homeless family whose child grew up to be an advocate for feeding the hungry, clothing the naked, and sheltering the homeless (Matthew 25)? I have a postcard of that sculpture resting on my desk as a haunting reminder of the indisputable anguish and sadness inherent in the birth of Jesus, as well as in every ensuing Christmas holiday...verily, in life itself.

We like to ameliorate the offensive reality of Jesus' birth, even as we desire to pacify the world's condition. But life is stark, often ugly and brutal. There was no room in the inn for baby Jesus then; there is seldom room in our modern hearts for the adult Jesus who advocated the hard and grueling message of peace and justice for all.

Finding no room in the inn and being born in a manger are grizzly reminders that the Prince of Peace, Emmanuel, Jesus wasn't born in splendor but rather in squalor. Which, of course, presages his mission, doesn't it? Jesus came not to traffic among the prominent or rich but instead to serve the weak, the outcast, and those living in poor and dreadful conditions not unlike where he was born.

That's the bedrock proclamation of Christmas. Whatever joy and peace and love you feel during the holidays, spread it abroad through serving the least, lost, and last of humanity. As Charles Dickens put it:

> We celebrate Christmas once again. God bless it!...It is required of everyone that the spirit within us should walk abroad among our human neighbors and travel far and wide. This is required by our joyful allegiance to the spirit of Jesus, a spirit sustained by the best in humanity ever since his day. The common welfare is our business; charity, mercy, forbearance are all our business...

Is the common welfare of humanity our actual business? Is universal compassion our supreme human mission? Is there room in our hearts for all the brothers and sisters of humankind? Those are the questions posed by the birth of Jesus, moreover, by the ministry of Jesus and reinforced by the testimony of Christmas novelist Charles Dickens whose own life was one of relentless commitment to charitable causes. Dickens believed, and so do I that the central business of Christmas is generosity.

"Sore Afraid!"

"The hopes and fears of all the years
are met in thee tonight."
—Phillip Brooks
(From the hymn "O Little Town of Bethlehem")

People habitually seek short-cuts to joy. I know I often do. The holidays are no exception, maybe even worse.

I don't know how many times I've read the Lucan story of the birth of Jesus and never thought seriously about the shepherd's initial response of fear, great fear, upon encountering the divine messenger out in the fields. They were shepherding, doing their job, and were abruptly interrupted by an extraordinary event. An angel appeared, "the glory of the Lord shone around them," and the shepherds were "filled with fear."

We reside in a different time-frame. Already aware of Jesus' birth, already privy to the angel's message, we moderns are off and running to the birthday celebration. We avoid any shock or surprise. We're so accustomed to hearing the comforting words that follow, "Be not afraid, for behold I bring you good news of a great joy…" that we forget the bona fide fear that must be soothed.

The shepherds were "sore afraid" reads the King James Version. So afraid, their beings were aching, sore. The New English Bible translates the phrase: "Terribly afraid." So we can see that the shepherds weren't just caught off guard, not merely unnerved or beset with a mild anxiety attack, but "sore afraid." Filled with fear, real scared.

Why? Who really knows? Frightened by the

startling voice of a strange personage? Frightened by a power beyond their control, a presence beyond their comprehension, an improbable event beyond their wildest anticipation? In any case, whatever the source, "they were sore afraid."

Now, as we all know, there's a dramatic and happy ending. The fears of the shepherds are, in fact, allayed. They go with haste to Bethlehem, see Mary, Joseph, and the babe lying in a manger, are duly impressed, spread the good news and return home "glorifying and praising God for all they had heard and seen."

But not, however, before they had to face full-fledged fear.

You may be asking: why is it important for 21st century religious folk to appreciate the fright of the ancient shepherds? My reply is plain and simple: because, guess what, we too are afraid of Christmas! Afraid at Christmas? What's there to fear during the holidays? Well, the same things we fear during the rest of the year, only they're more intense and magnified during December.

First off, there are the perennial December fears. December is loud and obnoxious. The noise decibels of children rise markedly. Raucous parties abound. Our ears and hearts are assaulted by crowds here, there, and everywhere. December is also a month of unceasing, pounding Muzak. In elevators and department stores, on TV, and when the telephone keeps us on hold, from loud speakers and hidden speakers and sometimes from no obvious place at all, we're bombarded by tape-recorded holiday mush. There's even the nasty rumor that Muzak will soon be piped into our city sewer systems.

I know, many of these same, delightful carols are played in our congregations and will be sung to house-bound elders during the holidays, but with one distinct, crucial advantage: we will be doing the singing ourselves! Unless, you don't like to hear your own voice; then that's an additional problem.

Another December fear is the fact that it's a hurried and hassled month. Too many decisions have to be made quickly. There's an endless stream of tantalizing pitches and mercantile hype at every juncture. Too much money is being spent, and end-of-the year bills are piling up and have to be met. December consistently puts the most strain on our family budget of any month. All in all, it's very unlikely that even the most stable and adroit among us will escape unscathed from a modicum of December dread.

Furthermore, there exist the notorious fears that seem to be aggravated during the holidays because of our heightened vulnerability. The American Psychiatric Association has identified the four as follows, any one of which might disrupt our spiritual serenity sometime during December.

The first fear is *leisure* or idle time that symbol of

vast emptiness and absence of the creative ties that bind reality together. Sounds a bit strange, but I think you can fathom the sneaky force of this potent fear.

Therapists see *loneliness* as another major worry. There's the symbol, yea reality, of abandonment even amidst the bustling throng. Everyone else in the pack seems to be connected, together...except you or I. We aren't linked, so we feel alone. Unless such accentuated holiday isolation is nipped in the bud, it can turn chronic and last all winter and beyond. Or catch us off-guard the ensuing December.

A third primary fear is *silence*. It's interesting, isn't it, how both empty quiet can cause anxiety as well as burdensome clatter? Silence represents the vividness of lost music, lost happy voices, lost dreams, and lost time...we're haunted by a painful stillness.

Finally, there is *death* that designates the nothingness, the agony of finality, the brink of an unknown eternity. And death is piercingly heightened during the holiday *joie de vivre*, especially when recalling the departure of loved ones.

At the first Christmas season, Matthew recalled the slaughter of innocents, the horrible episode that followed Jesus' birth. And now, in our contemporary world, slaughters occur all around us...with the slaughter of slaughters lurking: nuclear omnicide, the slaughter of innocent and culpable alike, the loss of all living entities, of everything.

Now, of course, you and I can transform leisure into beneficial creativity, loneliness into salubrious solitude, silence into a blessed communion, and death into the natural completion of a meaningful cycle. But that's no easy feat to accomplish amid the December maelstrom; and, before any such conversion can transpire, numerous, actual fears still persist and must be experienced before truly enjoying the birthday party in Bethlehem.

As one of our favorite Christmas carols declares, "The hopes and fears of all the years are met in thee tonight." Yes, hopes and fears, both, are met in thee, oh Christmas time.

Furthermore, our fears during the holidays arise not only because of demons such as loneliness and death but also because of "an angel of the Lord," who makes extraordinary and stressful demands upon our lives. The birth of a compassion-carrier like Jesus makes the human enterprise more joyous; yet, precisely because of his prophetic sting, Jesus also makes our lives more difficult, to say the least. In many ways, it would be much easier on all of humanity if Jesus hadn't arrived. For he came, as they say, not only to comfort the afflicted but also to afflict the comfortable!

Psychologists have long told us, and rightly so that we're attracted to the experiences we fear. We're often drawn to and terrorized by the very same things. For example, fire, freedom, adventure, and intimacy all both charm and terrify us. And how about "peace and good will among all," the two challenges laid at the shepherd's feet by the angel? Sound absolutely appealing, don't they? Just what we want, right?

Well, it's not so straightforward. The people of Jesus' era didn't ardently pursue genuine peace and authentic good will, did they? And we moderns have fared no better. Sometimes we seem, in fact, to have regressed when it comes to waging peace and incarnating good will, even in our own families, let alone international relations. Peace and good will would drive hate-mongers out of business, would end books of bigotry, would force preachers of ill-will and divisiveness out of their pulpits and teachers of prejudice out of their classroom, and peace and good will would add terrorists to the unemployed and ruin politicians who scheme to have truth compromised. Furthermore, peace and good will would deliver justice and mercy to the people in squalid slums, the refugees of urban renewal and economic devastation, as well as deliver liberation to the victims of violence and the children of hopelessness.

And if all that sounds a bit remote, then think of the direct and mighty effects of peace and good will in our daily lives. There's no doubt in my mind that peace and good will would turn us upside-down and inside-out. We desire them, we need them, yet we're sorely afraid of them, for they're too tough and taxing, too backbreaking and heartbreaking. They spell revolutionary shifts in the ways we feel, think, talk, and act at home and abroad. They require transformation.

We're also afraid of good will and peace, because, even when we sincerely pursue them, we perpetually fall short of reaching them, time after time. They ask for more than we seem to be able or willing to deliver. Jesus did his best 2,000 years ago. Other prophets of peace and good will have carried their fair share in the intervening years. And where are we today? Nearer or farther from universal peace and good will among people? We're as afraid of "peace and good will" as ever; we're afraid of daily failure and final failure. Nonetheless, religious people can never act as if failure is morally justified. The shaky fate of all that is sacred and worthy in life dare not intimidate us into inaction. Scare us, sure, but terrify us into paralysis, never. For the future belongs to persons of peace and good will. Because, without such bold pioneers and relentless prophets, there will be no future worth having.

The world, *our* world is still waiting for you and me not just to be ardent peace-lovers but also to dare to become forceful peacemakers. For as the Galilean rabbi put it in his own ministry: "Blessed are the peacemakers, for they shall be called the sons and daughters of God…" (Matthew 5:9) It helps to heed the actual Aramaic translation of "peacemaking," which means "planting peace every season." Clearly, being a genuine peacemaker is a far more demanding quest than merely being peaceable—accommodating, sweet, and nice. This much is certain: if we truly aspire to be peacemakers, not merely peace-seekers, we will never be out of work…at Christmas time or any other season of our lives!

It has been said that the best we can do in this world, in our lifetime, is to increase the odds of something more peaceful, more just, and more beautiful happening. Well, if increasing the odds is all we can accomplish, then let's go for it. Let's increase the odds with every ounce of imaginable courage and good deed.

But there's more to the birth narrative. If you and I have really heard, felt, and embodied the shepherd's fear, then let's also welcome the shepherd's robust rejoicing as well. The shepherd's delight was the "good news of a great joy which will come to all the people," namely, the good news that the Prince of Peace is on the way and will prod us toward peace all our days and nights…hence, fear isn't the whole story or the final word of existence. The good news of the holidays is that our fears can be eased, even if not eliminated, by love; our despair can be diminished by hope; and our cynicism can be shrunk by faithfulness.

There's another fascinating thing about this

encounter between the angel and the shepherds. Remember that the shepherds, merely doing their daily job on a rather dark and lonely hillside, were the first ones to hear about the birth of Jesus. They got the message before anyone else, and only after they were caught in the throes of feeling sore afraid.

Maybe that's the way it happens. Perhaps the messages of substantial and enduring good news come to us most powerfully and poignantly amidst our fears not our frivolity, when we're down rather than up, when least expected instead of thoroughly plotted out. What I'm suggesting is that those among us who know fear might just prove keenly receptive to knowing joy.

Although it's true that despondency strikes newcomers and old-timers alike during December, it's also true that greater suicide rates and high admission rates to mental hospitals at Christmas are inaccurate. The National Center for Health Statistics shows that the fewest suicides occur during December, when compared with other days during the year. Risks also decrease for New Year' Day, Independence Day, and Labor Day. Evidently the holidays, while bringing immense stress, also provide considerable psychological and social protection against suicide. As the carol heralds: "Faithful friends who are dear to us, gather near to us once more..." The gathering of relatives who visit from out of town, sometimes staying for several days, is likely to protect vulnerable people.

In sum, it's good to know that if you're joyous, it doesn't mean that you're just superficial or out of step, or if you're depressed that you're going to do something drastic or deadly. In fact, roughly ten out of ten people suffer "adverse emotional reactions" to life itself and frequently during the holidays. Even saints, maybe especially saints—agonize and anguish. So welcome to the largest fellowship in the universe: the fellowship of those who experience fear and feel pain during December.

My religion has persuaded me that during December, all of us are shepherds plying our trades out on dark and lonely hillsides, and we are often "sore afraid;" yet if we stay around long enough to hear the gospel of good will and peace, and stick around even longer to have those words become flesh in our lives, then some of the dark places will be lit up, and the humblest and most hurting among us can be nourished, even renewed.

When I was serving Fountain Street Church in Grand Rapids, Michigan, every Christmas Eve, Carol Kooistra, a long-time pillar of the congregation, would rise at the midnight service to sing *O Holy Night*. The service was seemingly incomplete without Carol's stunning, soulful rendition of this classic carol. However, in 2004, one week prior to Christmas, she had lost her beloved husband Bill to a lengthy bout with cancer. We gave Carol every possible "out," but she wouldn't hear of it. "I must sing *O Holy Night*; it will help me heal from this unspeakable loss. Bill would want me to rise up and sing from the depths of my grief and gratitude. And I'm not about to disappoint him or myself or my beloved congregation!"

A thrill of hope, the weary world rejoices, for yonder breaks a new and glorious morn. Fall on your knees, oh, hear the angel voices! Oh, night divine, O night when Christ was born! O night divine, oh night, oh night divine!

The Year they
Cancelled Christmas

"I will honor Christmas in my heart,
and try to keep it all the year."
—Charles Dickens

I want to relate a story, perhaps familiar in some version to most of us, yet a tale we rarely divulge this holiday time of the year. I first picked it up years back from Susan Rodd in an offbeat magazine article and share my own expanded perspective on this legend, undoubtedly a mixture of fact and fable.

As our trees sparkle with cherished ornaments, children are giddy with delight, and spicy cookies bake in our ovens every Christmas season, it's difficult to imagine a world with no Christmas at all. But it happened.

On June 3, 1647, British Parliament established punishments for anyone caught observing Christmas. In jolly olde England, the twelve days of Christmas had become the time for all good nobles and merchants to show their loyalty to the king by offering splendid gifts, including outright cash.

Gambling was also very fashionable at Christmas. Kings and Bishops would outdo each other in the splendor of their attire and the bounty of their banquets. Inevitably, there were reactions against these excesses, so when the puritanical Roundheads came to power, beheading King Charles I and establishing Oliver Lord Cromwell Lord Protector of the country, the edict banning Christmas occurred. Town criers passed through the streets ringing their bells and shouting, "No Christmas! No Christmas!"

Carol singing and broadsides (a sort of Christmas

card precursor) disappeared from public life. Plum puddings, caroling, and mistletoe were lost as well. Even the baking of mincemeat pie, a Christmas favorite, was outlawed. The poor were too oppressed to celebrate, and the wealthy didn't want to waste the time. So, Christmas became a full-force workday.

In England, folks soon found the years without Christmas to be intolerable. When the monarchy was restored in 1660, Christmas regained official acceptance once more. As the middle class rose, Christmas became more a celebration of the people and less an excuse for royal pomposity.

The squashing of Christmas had spread to the New World as well with merrymaking losses comparable to those suffered in England. However, America took longer to recover from the cheerless, oppressive Puritan influence. In 1856 Christmas Day was still an ordinary workday in Boston, and failure to report to a job was grounds for dismissal. Fortuitously, the influence of immigrants from Germany and Ireland finally persuaded Yankees that Christmas could be a risk-free, even religious, festivity. The first state to declare Christmas a legal holiday was Alabama in 1836. The last was Oklahoma in 1890.

There was a counter-crier in England who set out to advocate the honorable merits and compassionate merriment of Christmas. *A Christmas Carol* (1843) by Charles Dickens, next to the nativity itself, remains the best known and loved Christmas story of all. It's the ultimate embodiment of what Dickens himself called:

> *The Carol philosophy; that Christmas is a good time, a kind, forgiving, charitable, pleasant time, the only time I know of, in the long calendar of the year, when men and women seem by one consent to open their shut-up hearts freely, and to think of other people below them as if they really were fellow passengers to the grave and not another race of creatures found on their journeys.*

Dickens' efforts succeeded, and Christmas has survived and blooms year after year, both within our hearts and in the air. As we bask in the recovery of this healthy, hearty, and holy season every December, may we stand in alignment with the supreme compliment paid to the reformed Scrooge: "And it was always said of him that he knew how to keep Christmas well, if anyone alive possessed the knowledge. May that be truly said of us, and all of us! And so, as Tiny Tim observed, God bless us, every one!" Dickens' vision of Christmas contends that joy need not turn hedonistic that giving need not be fake or bribery, and that savoring life need not be incompatible with serving it.

It's tempting and easy to righteously dump on all the holiday hoopla. And we do. Preachers rail against its mercenary excesses. Psychologists remind us that it can lead to disorders of anxiety and depression. Sociologists say that it can disrupt family life. Rationalists clamor that it's merely ancient superstition celebrated on the wrong date.

But life-affirming, cheerful folks refuse to allow anyone to ruin the annual Christmas revelry. We have little enough joy in the world, little enough sacred time and space, little enough genuine compassion, little enough feast, festival, and fantasy as it is to permit the Scrooges of the planet to diminish, let alone ban, the holiday.

Religious revelers choose to unwrap the inner gifts of Christmas!

Giving from the Heart

"Those folks who have not Christmas in their
hearts will never find it under a tree."
—Roy L. Smith

Recognizing the excesses and abuses of the Christmas season, we are, nonetheless, spurred to represent humanity at our most kind-hearted. Here are a few reminders to strike the middle way between the hyper-commercialism of medieval England and contemporary America and the rampant cynicism that spurns the spark of joy bursting in our hearts.

Lesson #1: give gifts that are real not rote, fresh not stale. Someone gave a Christmas card simply because she thought she "should." As the story goes, she dashed into the Hallmark store at the local mall, grabbed a box of 50 innocuous looking cards, and without reading the message, scribbled 49 to all the people in her address book that she didn't expect to see over the holiday season. Sound familiar?

A day or two later, when the cards were well into the mail, she chanced upon the one card that had not been sent. Perhaps you can imagine her horror when she read, "This card is just to say…a little gift is on the way." Our friend here did what she felt was obligatory and got caught, because she hurried too fast. She did something that she didn't really care about, something she had been constrained to believe she had to do. In sum, if you don't mean it, don't do it. Societal pressure often leads to poor choices. Pause and remind yourself that you are giving because you have an option. Give from your heart.

Lesson #2: Gift-giving is spiritually vital only if we are responsive receivers as well. That may be the subtle key. Giving generously must be matched up with receiving gratefully. So let's find ways and moments during the season to be merry, exuberant receivers. Too many of us who are mighty good at giving aren't so hot at receiving, but the religious imperative is to be bilateral, to grow increasingly mature at both delivering and garnering gifts, surprises, and blessings. Why not start being "ambidextrous" during the Christmas season?

In truth, there can be no full giving without satisfied receiving. They are yoked. Ultimately gift-giving is a relationship, and just as the act of giving produces spiritual connection, so too does the act of receiving. As I often say during the time of Offertory: "Some say it is more blessed to give than to receive, and others say, nay, it's more blessed to receive than to give. But we affirm that which is truly blessed when we give from a generous, genuine heart, and, when we receive that we receive with grateful, open arms. Giving and receiving are both holy acts!"

Lesson #3: as we meander through the marvels and messes of December, we would be wise to remain attentive to the sacred in the ordinary or the holy in the mundane. Let joy crack open amidst the most conventional of our daily events. Remember joy is an unmerited surprise, so, if we stay spiritually awake, we may be (alas, no promises) showered during December with a sprig or spray of life-giving radiance. Jesus, throughout his ensuing career of boundless compassion, reminded us that the realm of God dwells in the midst of us, right where we live, not behind or beyond or above us.

It all started on Christmas day, didn't it, with the birth of Emmanuel, which literally means "God with us"? From Christmas day forward, we should acknowledge, in our innermost beings that the Eternal is present in everyday events and emotions, not just in the extraordinary ones.

Treat the holidays as if every moment or thing matters as a potential carrier of grace. Don't just show up emotionally for the planned festivities or parties during the holidays. If anything, decline a few of those. Instead, open your heart wide to the daily astonishments that reside right in front of you. Otherwise, you might miss the preciousness of an unruly child or ignore the novel insight from an old carol.

Lesson #4: we need to quit fretting about finding or giving the perfect gift. Give from your soul and worry not about whether it's a fine, even fitting, let alone perfect, gift. Remember that special gifts are often unexpected ones. At this time of the year, popular magazines are sporting articles about "The Perfect Gift" for the season, pushing their products shamelessly. Don't believe them; no gift is absolutely perfect, but there are sufficiently good gifts.

My colleague, Peter Heinrichs offers a few words in favor of the imperfect gift. It's a story that could pretty much be told about my own grandmother Zelma Flanagan and myself—not exactly, but the loving sensibility is quite comparable. Indeed, I bet many of you will also identify with this tale of the imperfect gift. Rev. Heinrichs relates:

One day after my grandmother died years ago, I took part in the sad but fascinating ritual of breaking up her household. I worked on the breakfast room. The room had a sunny, quiet, affectionate feel to it, unlike the austere formality of the dining and living rooms. My grandmother was fond of her morning moments in the breakfast room. And objects she was particularly fond of gravitated there with her.

At about eye level on one of the shelves stood an object that didn't seem at home there. It was a glass candy dish. Painted hot pink, and laminated with odd cabbage-like bumps on the dish cover and three skimpy legs below. It was hideous. Now where, I thought, did this thing come from? It was so unlike Grandma, whose tastes ran to bone china and rosewood. Why would she keep such a thing?

And then I remembered. I had given her the dish for Christmas nearly 30 years before. It had been an extravagance on my part, taking up a good part of the ten dollars or so I had saved for presents for family and friends. I was an 8-year-old. I was very proud of the dish because I had chosen it and bought it myself. I was attempting, awkwardly to be sure, to symbolize my love for my Grandma through (an adult) gift.

Now, if I had been my grandmother, receiving such a present, I probably would have conspicuously displayed the thing on the living room mantel for the holidays then discretely chucked it. But she kept it among her cherished things. Perhaps she did so precisely because of the awkwardness of the fit. Perhaps she kept it as a sign that her oldest grandchild was growing up. Perhaps it reminded her of her own childhood. Perhaps it simply warmed her heart, for love seldom comes in perfect packages.

Yes, Christmas often comes in the guise of a glass candy dish, painted hot pink and laminated with odd cabbage-like bumps on the dish cover and three skimpy legs below. Hideous, to be sure, yet a gift offered from the loving heart of an eight-year-old. Love dwells at the heart of clumsy, flawed gifts delivered with foibled yet overflowing affection.

I never knew my grandfathers John and Frank; they were gone when I was but a baby, the former from a heart attack in his late forties and the latter from a tragic suicide. And so, I never really knew what it would be like to be a grandfather myself; yet I've been learning fast on the job, day by day, ever since our first, Trevor, was born on January 26, 1996.

Once at an intergenerational holiday tree trimming potluck at our Church, I got to racing around our patio, chasing our two grandchildren, Trevor nearly four, and Corinne, just two. When I finally caught up with Trevor, we mutually embraced in zany delight and delivered our customary kiss on each other's nose. Not a peck, but more or less a playful, slobbery nibble, if you know what I mean—a clear-cut imperfect gift if there ever was one, but our own homegrown, precious ritual. For, as Emerson wrote: "the best gift is a gift of thyself," and our kisses surely qualify!

Adrift in Irony

"God gave Moses the Ten Commandments and
then He gave Irving Berlin…White Christmas."
—Philip Roth

This piece discloses my own thoughts sparked by Jody Rosen's splendid biography (2002) of Irving Berlin entitled *White Christmas: The Story of an American Song.* Of all the holiday music, no song is played more frequently or sung more lustily than Irving Berlin's *White Christmas.* The estimates of its record sales tally around 400 million copies. Berlin first considered it a "throwaway" satirical number for a vaudeville show; yet after he had finally brought it to light, Berlin rated *White Christmas* as his finest song. Here are some snapshots of the ambiguities rife in the development of this classic.

Berlin, a musical genius who couldn't script his own music, arose early one morning and burst in upon his musical notator, Helmy Kresa, declaring: "I want you to take down a song I wrote over the weekend (January, 1940). Helmy, it's not only the best song I ever wrote, it's the best song anybody ever wrote." It's hard to argue with the buoyant, oft-brash Berlin.

Skirting the unbridled cheerfulness of most yuletide tunes, *White Christmas* is a pensive song that yearns for the vanished past. The narrator is aching for Christmases "just like the ones I used to know." He's dreaming and invites us to follow suit.

Berlin was born Israel Baline in western Siberia in 1888. At the age of five his family navigated a most arduous, risky trek to the New World from the shtetl of Tyumen. *White Christmas* unveils the fantasy of a New

York expatriate stranded in Beverly Hills (you'll recall that Berlin straddled both coasts with residences in each) during the winter.

As a young boy, growing up in Pasadena, California, I never saw snow first-hand until one January morn in 1951 (I was just 9 years old) when it snowed. This was a startling, unheard-of Southern California occurrence, so bizarre that school was called off at noon, and we all raced home to frolic in the snow. My brother and I immediately built a snowman in our front yard, went in for a hot lunch prepared by Mom, then returned outdoors, only to find that Frosty had shriveled into a pool of water.

When I shared this episode recently with my older brother Phil, he reminded me of two additional elements: first off, it was his very birthday on January 9, 1951, so this unusual blast of hail and sleet was an especially hallowed occasion for Phil as a newly-minted 12-year-old. Secondly, the "snow fall" stuck long enough for him to recall that one of our childhood neighbors, Betsy Birdsey, had launched a snowball that struck Phil directly in the stomach, and that he had chased Betsy all the way home, flinging snowball after snowball, to no avail, as Betsy scooted safely into her abode. By the way, did you know that *Frosty the Snowman* was written only one year earlier in 1950?

Another irony: so many of America's most beloved holiday songs from Felix Bernard's *Winter Wonderland*

(1934) to Mel Torme's *The Christmas Song* (1944), to Sammy Cahn and Jule Styne's *Let it Snow* (1945) to Johnny Marks' *Rudolph the Red-Nosed Reindeer* (1948) to Al Stillman's *Home for the Holidays* (1954) to Jerry Herman's *We Need a Little Christmas* (1966) to Sheldon Harnick's (who, by the way, wrote the lyrics for the classic *Fiddler on the Roof* in 1964) *Christmas Gifts* (1989) were created by Jews, outsiders who wrote themselves into the center of musical life in America. Then, most recently, there's Barry Alan Pincus, born in 1943 of Jewish lineage, known to one and all as Barry Manilow. In 1990, he wrote a poignant holiday song entitled *Because It's Christmas*. These prolific Jewish composers and lyricists often specialized in holiday music, producing numerous ballads for Christmas-time. And I'm sure my list is leaving someone out.

Irving Berlin himself was the son of an Orthodox Jewish cantor. But as he put it: "Christmas has woven a pattern in my life." When pressed "how could a Jew write it," Berlin confidently replied: "I know how. I wrote it as an American." Remember it was Izzy Berlin who also wrote "God Bless America." A Russian-Jewish immigrant became perhaps the premier pop songwriter of his adopted country.

Although the ever-cocky and brilliant Berlin considered *White Christmas* a sure-fire hit, it went unnoticed until American GI's embraced Bing Crosby's rendition as an improbable wartime anthem. Piped into the barracks, it struck a wistful and responsive chord for soldiers facing perhaps their initial holiday overseas. The words have nothing to do with wartime, but it goes right to the heart of nostalgia. You can only imagine the intensity of men and women pining for hearth and home. This sensibility is echoed in other holiday music as well: *I'll be Home for Christmas* ("if only in my dreams").

Oh, the colors of the holidays: red, green, white, blue, and more... there's the red of Rudolph the red-nosed reindeer, the green of old Tannenbaum and mistletoe, the white of this frosty season, and the blues experienced in many a psyche. There's an inescapable melancholy that riddles *White Christmas*. The words aren't as blatantly sad as in *Blue Christmas*, yet it has a downright bluesy feel to it. Which reminds one of the intertwining blue and white colors of Hanukkah.

A final ironic twist. The lyrics capture the heart of Berlinian simplicity. Forty-four of its fifty-three words are but one syllable words. The rhymes are elementary. *White Christmas* is utterly ingenuous and straightforward, yet deeply profound, both in lyric and melody. As Berlin would phrase it: "A simple melody will always linger. I mean the kind you pick out with one finger." It was, perchance, composed with one finger, but sung with one's entire body and soul!

"Can You Jolly It Up a Bit?"

"At Christmas, all roads
lead home."
—MARJORIE HOLMES

A local San Diego newspaper story by John Wilkens has sparked this reflective essay.

Songwriter Hugh Martin's *Have Yourself a Merry Little Christmas* has been a holiday classic for 70+ years. Martin died just a couple years ago at the ripe age of 96, living quietly in our hometown of San Diego. Hugh Martin was a superb performer, arranger, and composer who was elected to the Songwriter's Hall of Fame in 1983, although he was bedeviled with lifelong bouts of low self-esteem.

Along with his partner Ralph Blane, Martin was assigned to write songs for the movie "Meet Me in St. Louis," starring Judy Garland. The lyrics he wrote were sad, exceedingly sad. They were composed for the Judy Garland character to sing to her younger sister, who was in tears about the family moving from Missouri to New York City. "Have yourself a merry little Christmas, it may be your last," the original began. "Next year we may all be living in the past." And later, "Faithful friends who were dear to us, will be near to us no more." The movie executives, upon hearing it, agreed: "Well, it's okay for the song to be bittersweet and nostalgic, but it shouldn't be a dirge," according to an account Martin includes in his autobiography *Hugh Martin: The Boy Next Door.*

Garland initially refused to sing *Have Yourself a Merry Little Christmas* in the 1943 movie, because she considered it too gloomy. At first Martin declined to change the lyrics. "Tell Judy if she wants the melody, she's gotta take the lyric," he angrily told a spokesperson. Martin soon relented to change the lyrics. And the ensuing version Garland recorded went: "Have yourself a merry little Christmas, let your heart be light; from now on our troubles will be out of sight." Other hopeful touches were added along the way.

Released during World War II, the song became a favorite among soldiers aching for home. "Judy was right, if I'd kept the lyrics the way they were, it would have been thrown out and forgotten," Hugh confessed. Fourteen years later, he changed the song again, for Frank Sinatra this time. "Can you jolly it up a bit?" Sinatra pressed. And Martin responded with "hang a shining star upon the highest bough" instead of "until then, we'll have to muddle through somehow."

Most singers have agreed with the Sinatra revision, but contemporary folk artist James Taylor thought "muddle through somehow" better fit the mood of our modern world. Indeed, perhaps it does. As Bette Midler once said, upon including the song in her own 2006 holiday album: "This holiday song manages to be happy and sad at the same time, hopeful but full of melancholy."

Other holiday songs reflect this blend of hope and despair, delight and difficulty as well. For example, the "I Heard the Bells on Christmas Day" carol starts by proclaiming: "I heard the bells on Christmas day, their old familiar carols play, and wild and sweet the words repeat, of peace on earth good will to all." But shortly thereafter, a different picture is portrayed of the current world: "And in despair I bowed my head; 'there is no peace on earth', I said, for hate is strong and mocks the song, of 'peace on earth, good will to all.'"

Well, what was the context of this 1863 poem entitled *Christmas Bells*, penned by Henry Wadsworth Longfellow? During the long dark years of the Civil War, there were millions of weary hearts in America anxiously awaiting the dawn of peace. The illustrious American poet Longfellow had personal experience with the tragedy of war. He knew first-hand the gloom of war's darkest hours. His young son, a lieutenant in the Army of the Potomac, had been seriously wounded in battle. Several entries in Longfellow's journal make reference to the war alongside his fervent and abiding hope that it might have a speedy end. So he wrote this powerful poem as a catharsis.

In rhythmic fashion, the carol triumphs in the final verse:

> *Then pealed the bells more loud and deep, God is not dead, nor doth God sleep! The wrong shall fail, the right prevail, with peace on earth, good will to all.*

And Jerry Herman, of *Hello Dolly* and *Mame* fame,

caught our holiday's intractable ambiguity, compos-
ing, in a considerably lighter vein, his own 1966
holiday ballad: *We Need a Little Christmas...* "For I've
grown a little leaner, grown a little colder, grown a
little sadder, grown a little older. And I need a little
angel, sitting on my shoulder, need a little Christmas
now." There are thirteen references to "little" in the
carol, so his message is unmistakable. Herman's summons evidently isn't for a gigantic or overpowering
Christmas but just for a *little* one. Is that all we truly
need or is it a cautionary plea not to overdo it during
the holiday? Or do both sentiments hold true?

In any case, Martin's *Have Yourself a Merry Little
Christmas* concludes with just the proper amount of
jollity, hope, and love. Not too much, not too little;
Christmas requires just the right mix. "Joy and sadness are woven fine," as the poet Blake writes. Strikes
me as precisely the way Christmas usually sleighs into
town.

Gift: Bribe or Blessing?

"The best of all gifts around any Christmas tree
is the presence of a happy family all
wrapped up in each other."
—Burton Hillis

When you're living in a different land and learning a new language you often hear words or portions of words that sound just like your own native tongue and, for a moment, you feel blessed with a piece of the familiar amidst the foreign. Soon after my arrival in Germany in 1968, I was amazed (since I was just beginning to learn German!) to hear a word pronounced and spelled no less just like an English word. The word was "gift," and you know what it means in German? *Poison!*

So, whenever I hear or use the word "gift" now, across my mind flashes, "Beware, poison!" As if that vivid association is not enough to startle my awareness, I recently came across four definitions of the words "gift" in Webster's Dictionary. Lo and behold, last but not least, reads: "Obs. A bribe." Well, this definition of gift may be obsolete, but the reality certainly isn't. A good many of our gifts during the holidays are offered not as presents but as blackmail.

Our gifts often come with strings attached or arrive as guilt payments and occasionally lead to broken dreams, lingering resentments, and obligatory binds. As Colman McCarthy writes:

> *"Christmas becomes the season of making up, especially to the kids, via store bought litter, all the emotional support that is absent between Christmases…it is a buy-off!" Or as Webster put it, "a bribe."*

However, gifting is here to stay, and I'm glad, for gifting can be a mutually enriching and gratifying enterprise for all concerned, if, as D. H. Lawrence phrased it, our giving "means kindling the life quality where it is not." That's a large "if," but a crucial and manageable "if" for us to ensoul through our holidays.

We can start by asking and answering some key questions: beyond personal necessities, what would I truly love, not just like, to receive this December? What kind of gift would I really desire to unwrap under the tree? It might be a spiritual gift or a relational present rather than something material. How would I celebrate the holidays if I had no or little money to spend on gifts? How can I help some people whom I may not even know be a bit merrier during this season? Is there something (not store-bought) that we can make or share together as a family that would have special meaning?

If we try to gift imaginatively and lovingly, from the deeper zones of our generosity, we are less likely to be victimized by the seasonal malaise. I don't know about you, but I'm at my jolliest during December when I give additional money to community causes in need, when I go out of my way to visit someone ill, when I assist in the conversion of a scrooge, or when I sing carols with unsuspecting folks.

Let's find those holiday places where we hallow and are hallowed, then show up bearing *and* baring gifts of our souls....inner gifts that promise to be blessings rather than bribes.

"Repeat the Sounding Joy"

"Christmas isn't a season.
It's a feeling."
—EDNA FERBER

I find myself when mid-November approaches shelving my regular songbooks and plunging straightway into my cherished holiday book filled with some 60 plus carols, replete with stories behind the yuletide ballads.

I retreat to my corner in the living room, pick up my KCE-26 Taylor guitar and strum the chords and croon the melodies of each carol, one by one, since I can't think of any I don't relish in one way or another. Here are some of the phrases that help me navigate the hard days and nights of December; indeed, enabling my heart to reverberate more gleefully during the upcoming year.

- from *Christmas Bells are Ringing*
  "Joyous voices sweet and clear, sing the sad of heart to cheer. Ding, dong, ding, dong, Christmas bells are ringing." I know it sounds quirky and mystical, but I can often hear bells, as I warble. I also harbor both a tambourine and hand chimes nearby to render additional joyful noise. When I do so, I'm heeding my Hebraic forerunners by "making a joyful noise to God, all the earth..." including my own soul and whoever might dwell in the vicinity.

- from *The Christmas Song*
  "And so, I'm offering this simple phrase to kids

from one to ninety-two, although it's been said many times, many ways, Merry Christmas to you!"

I remember vividly, celebrating Christmas Eve in 2003 (commemorating Dad's death as well) with Mom, my brother and me, just the three of us lounging on the couch in the living room of her modest duplex. Phil and I would sing carol after carol after carol, crooning every last refrain of my Mom's favorite Christmas music. Lamentably, I never heard my Mom's actual singing voice, since she quit singing as a young girl, when her school teacher, reinforced by her own parents, declared: "Mary, you don't sing on tune!" Nonetheless, although Mary Catherine Flanagan never opened her mouth to sing again since childhood, she still exulted in the carols, especially when her two boys were singing to her, albeit, on that particular Christmas Eve without the serenading of her hubby's gorgeous tenor voice.

And then, one of my holiday delights, make that life-highlights, occurred on another earlier Christmas Eve (1996), when Mom who was in her nineties by then, sat with our first grandson on her lap—Trevor, who was approaching one—and alongside our entire San Diego clan singing *The Christmas Song*, vividly aware of the "simple phrase to kids from one to ninety–two." I'll never forget how closely our ages, from baby to great-grandmother, resembled the lyric of this legendary ballad.

- from *Deck the Halls*
  "...tis the season to be jolly, don we now our gay apparel," I'm reminded, not only of my gay friends, but, moreover, I make sure that I'm wearing my gaudy Christmas tie that shines and shivers, a tie that Carolyn bought some 20 years ago in a garage sale for a couple bucks. One of our grandchildren has already said: "Grandpa, I want that tie someday!" And I have to calm him down, saying: "Someday, my beloved, but not yet, not yet, not yet! I still like it, and it likes me!

- from *Jingle-Bell Rock*
  "What a bright time, it's the right time to rock the night away..." This rockabilly version of *Jingle Bells*, released in 1957 during my teenage years and the height of the rock-and-roll era sends my body to gamboling and my spirit to soaring. There's no way to keep still when belting out this Bobbie Helms' rouser.

- And let's not forget *Joy to the World*
  "Repeat the sounding joy, repeat the sounding joy, repeat, repeat the sounding joy." This phrase reminds me of Bach's classic advice for all budding

songsters and musicians to practice the scales of rejoicing, every day of one's life, in order to stay in sound vocal, but moreover, sound spiritual shape.

And I do, I do. I make some sort of music every day I draw breath...

The Story of Two Jameses

"Christmas is not a time nor a season, but a
state of mind. To cherish peace and goodwill,
to be plenteous in mercy, is to have
the real spirit of Christmas."
—CALVIN COOLIDGE

My Christmas Eve sharing tonight (1986) focuses on separate narratives about two persons who have struggled to bring joy, light, and meaning out of the murky foreboding of their lives. Both were named James; one dwelt in the early 19th century and the other lives today.

The story of the first James, James Pierpont, is simply yet masterfully recounted in a children's story by The Rev. Denise Tracy. Here are some snippets.

James Pierpont had been a failure at everything he tried. He'd run away from home at age fourteen to become a sailor and to seek his fortune. He found adventure but no fortune. He'd tried panning for gold, but after months of rich dreams, he had just the dreams and none of the gold.

James drifted about. His older brother was a minister in Savannah, Georgia, so he traveled there. It just so happened that the church was without a musician. James asked his brother to hire him, and his brother agreed.

Late one night James was practicing at the church. He'd gone over the hymns, the prelude and postlude. He was ready for Sunday. His mind filled with images. He'd been raised in New England, the son of a famous Unitarian Minister. James Pierpont came from a family that supported the abolition of slavery. He, himself, supported the South.

James could not go home to Boston. The slavery issue was a tense one for his family. Sitting in the quiet church he thought about New England and how he loved and missed it there.

Suddenly music and words filled his mind. He played and sang:
>Dashing through the snow
>in a one horse open sleigh
>o'er the fields we go
>laughing all the way.
>
>Bells on bobtails ring
>making spirits bright
>what fun it is to ride and sing,
>a sleighing song tonight.
>
>Jingle bells, Jingle Bells,
>jingle all the way,
>oh what fun it is to ride
>on a one horse open sleigh.

Here was James Pierpont, a man who failed at most things he tried, who wrote the words and music to a favorite tune most people know, as well known *and beloved as any carol in the world.*

But it was only in 1969 that it was discovered that James, not his famous father, John, had actually written this song.

So, James Pierpont, who failed at most things, overshadowed by his father, finally succeeded in bringing joy to the hearts of many people who sing Jingle Bells, Christmas after Christmas after Christmas.

The second James was a distraught and disheveled young man who visited our First Church years back. He attended sporadically, then moved on. He was bright, even visionary, yet emotionally disabled. And what made it tougher on everybody, especially James himself, was that he often knew it. I saw James one holiday (the holidays always exacerbated his issues) dressed like Jesus, preaching like Jesus, claiming to be Jesus, down in front of the San Diego Public Library. Neither of us was particularly comfortable in spotting one another under such circumstances, so our eyes quickly averted.

Next time Carolyn and I heard from James, he was in jail, followed by a mental hospital, then he returned to our parish briefly, as brilliant and bedeviled as ever. Then, a year or so later, we received a Christmas card from James from a mental hospital in his home state of Minnesota where, on his leaves, he unfailingly visited one of our Unitarian Universalist fellowships there.

An abused child, a troubled youth, now a tormented adult, James struggled mightily to bring order out of his chaos. James was always aspiring to sculpt meaning from his anguish. Now, this particular holiday season, James was toiling to deliver a gift to his world. His wasn't the gift of song as was the gift of the first James. Rather his was a visionary gift of peace for our universe, especially for abused and oppressed kids, since he had so little peace as a child and had garnered too little peace ever since.

From his mental hospital headquarters, James had founded "The World Children's Party" and composed a simple yet moving Children's Bill of Rights to accomplish, as he puts it, "healthier children and a superior world family."

James personally had never experienced most of the rights he fervently advocated. He had been robbed of them, but now, still depressed and down, James marshaled his interior might and savvy, calling upon us all to give the children of our globe the gifts they really needed this holiday...indeed, every day of their lives: gifts that lifted the spirit and strengthened the body, nourished the mind and motivated the conscience, gifts that healed and empowered rather than harmed and weakened.

James was crying out to American society: if you really love children, America, then love them. Don't abuse or coddle them. Don't rot their teeth or warp their minds or twist their spirits. Don't smother them with guilt or fear or junk. Give them the gifts they covet and never got. True gifts, lasting gifts, precious gifts.

In his Christmas card James invited Carolyn and me to read a brief poem that he wrote to our congregation on Christmas Eve. So, here is a portion:

*The hope of our world should be the peace of our children, for they are the most valuable resource we can **mine**. They are the most valuable resource we can **find**. They are the most valuable resource we can **choose**. They are the most valuable resource we can **love**.*

So stop the war before it starts and listen to our children's hearts.

Tonight, I chose not to retell the story of Jesus *birth*, but instead recounted the stories of James and James, stories of *rebirth*. Triumphant stories of two young adults, struggling and down, who, each in their own way, dared to become bringers of love in the midst of hostility and hope in the midst of despair.

James befuddled by failure, rose up to create music of joy.

James beset with demons, rises up to pen an emancipation proclamation for the beleaguered, little ones of the world.

When the outside is at its gloomiest and most frigid, our insides rise up and create the most joyous, peaceful loving festival of the year. Christmas has never existed for the smug or satisfied, but instead it exists for those who hanker to light yet another candle because the dark within and without is so great.

Christmas is sustained by the Jameses of our universe.

Will the Real Santa Claus Please Wink?

"I came across a study conducted by psychologists from Harvard and Yale that may shed light on the age-old question: How does Santa Claus do it? How does he keep fit year after year despite a breakneck schedule?

"Santa Claus, after all, is overweight, smokes a pipe, and lives on a diet of cookies and milk (whole milk, not skim). How does he do it?

"It's probably all that giving and caring—and those people depending on him—that keeps him such a healthy and happy old elf."

—BRUCE T. MARSHALL

The day before Thanksgiving I was in the North Park Shopping Mall in Davenport, Iowa and blaring out of the speakers came a tune that I knew I knew from somewhere: "You better watch out, you better not pout, you better not cry, I'm telling you why…Santa Claus is coming to town!"

It shouldn't have surprised me. Every year, before the turkey's in the oven, the tinsel's on its way up the tree. But I was still caught off guard and annoyed at this incredibly early mention of Santa Claus. I hadn't even had a chance to greet the Pilgrims, and old St. Nick was already sledding into town. Fast forward to 2013; before Halloween candy has been distributed, Christmas cards and decorations have already been placed for sale in stores.

Many of us have an uncomfortable awareness about this materialistic monster: America's very own golden calf. Already trapped with the chubby-cheeked Santa Claus as part of our family life, some of us try to rationalize his existence, others try to explain him out of our lives, and yet others find themselves in a highly conflicted state of mixed generosity and miserliness at Christmas time that all too often leads to being worn out, even spiritually bankrupt, by the 25th of December.

Therefore, one who has a grip as powerful as this fellow has on the American psyche commands closer scrutiny. Santa Claus is one myth that we Americans, ostensibly more than any other folk, seem to have taken quite seriously (even if not accurately). What has been selected, deleted, and spun into our own version of this myth tells us a great deal about who we are, what we value, and where we're headed as a nation.

What Santa Claus is doing to our children is not perhaps even as momentous as what he is doing to us adults, our larger culture. For it is the grown-ups who essentially own the purse strings, run the society, and shape or misshape the ideals and visions of contemporary life. One of my fellow elders, in a nursing home where I sing, playfully puts it this way: "When I was young, I believed in Santa Claus; as a youth, I rejected Santa Claus; now as a white-bearded old guy, I've become Santa Claus! Go figure!"

For starters, historical data is minimal. What we're left primarily with are legends from mythic material. But here are some useful and compelling notes I've culled, then modified, from Irving Cady of Alpena, Michigan. I'm sure you can google, to your mind's delight, more about Santa Claus.

Santa Klause, sometimes known as Kriss Kringle, had his origin in St. Nicholas (326-352) a highly popular saint of the Roman Catholic Church. He was a Bishop in Myra, Asia Minor. We also have some evidence that in 1087 Italian merchants and sailors set out to take his body from his tomb in Asia Minor, now ravaged by war, and place it in a new shrine in Bari, Italy.

For the next 1600 years after his death St. Nicholas, embellished by the imagination and devotion of certain folks, is pictured in iconography, songs, and plays as a person who knew above all else how to give.

These stories tell of perhaps the most popular saint in the history of Christianity: the ultimate gift-giver who expected nothing in return for his good deeds; in fact, he gave "so that the right hand didn't know what the left hand was doing."

There are several fascinating, pertinent narratives about St. Nicholas. One time he was begging grain from passing merchant ships to feed his starving people during a famine. Bishop Nicholas promised the sailors that at the final weighing in on their return home, not an ounce would be missing. He was also a special friend to children and therefore baked bread with sugar and spices from exotic lands and personally handed these breads out to children. The first gingerbread persons were made in Nick's image and likeness.

Another story out of this famine time tells of three wandering students, mere children, who were robbed, killed, and pickled in a vat by a desperate and cruel innkeeper. Nicholas found this out and restored all three to life. One sees this story depicted on ancient church walls even today in Europe. Over and over again: three children, rising from the vat and singing the praises of Nicholas as he blesses them.

Robbers were of special concern to Saint Nicholas. In fact, the association was so natural that much later, in England, thieves were referred to as "clerks of St. Nicholas" (See *Henry VIII* by Shakespeare). A stained glass window in Chartres, France shows the Saint giving clemency to a burglar. One is reminded of Christ, crucified between two thieves, one of them repenting and receiving promise of eternal glory.

As a representative of the Creator, it's not surprising that barren women invoked him as their special patron, hoping for a child. An old way of saying that a woman was pregnant was to say, "She has been to see St. Nicholas."

Several stories tell of Nicholas appearing in dreams and insisting on justice and the correction of false accusations. Perhaps this influences the "corrector" and "inspector" aspects of Nicholas that are conveyed even to this day in the holiday ditty: "He knows if you've been bad or good, so be good for goodness sake."

Then there are fables and icons that tell of a sailboat caught in a terrible storm. The sailors prayed for help and a figure appeared, giving courage and help with the sails and the ropes, and in an instant the storm is calmed. The ship harbors safely in Myra, and the sailors offer thanks in the church. There they recognize that it was Nicholas who saved them. In sum, bankers, pawnbrokers, girls hoping to marry, women hoping for children, sailors, boat makers, vat makers, thieves, prisoners, and children all claimed his special patronage.

St. Nicholas was mighty, noble, and at the core both compassionate and humane. He was a generous, secretive, unconditional gift-giver. But, as with any legendary saint, eventually he became distorted to fit the prevailing mentality and mythology of an era, even a country. As faith in the inner reference wanes, a phony substitute in the outer world is produced. As spiritual depth deteriorates, mercenary grab takes over.

Enter Madison Avenue. Water down all the profound aspects of this religiously powerful figure. Dress him up in a red snowsuit. Change his pointed bishop's miter for a fool's cap, and let him chuckle his way into our hearts. Until he comes across as the "Beat

Generation" poet Lawrence Ferlinghetti depicted him in the 1950's:

A fat handshaking stranger in a red flannel suit and a fake white beard who goes around passing himself off as some sort of North Pole saint...bearing sacks of Humble Gifts from Saks Fifth Avenue for everybody's imagined Christ child...

Enough on the history and legends of St. Nick. How about some of my own biases concerning this inimitable character?

First, we've interpreted this kindly Bishop of yesteryear to be not simply an Advent saint, which he surely was, but a savior, which he wasn't. Not a model for our own behavior, which he was, but a rescuer from afar off. Instead of having a modest "feast day" to honor his death on December 6th, and recounting his story as one who blessed those at sea and distributed gifts to the needy, we've converted St. Nicholas into a magical character whose munificence promises to solve most, if not all, of our holiday, as well as human, ills.

Our children want, and *we* want. But year after year, when Santa fails to deliver, mistrust and disappointment ensue.

As Psychologist Renzo Sereno states: "Many instances of total recall of an early experience with

Santa, once analyzed, reveal only fear, loneliness, and lack of faith in parental love."

Who hasn't skedaddled through the mine-field of Christmas where our children start fighting over who got what? A parent or grandparent is likely to recoil in shock at all this greed on the birthday of the Prince of Peace. But it's understandable, isn't it? Children are tussling for the love of their families, and they don't care to share one bit of it, especially when there seems to exist a limited supply in the house. Many children don't handle this crisis successfully and, years later, may tell their "shrink" of the deep hatred they had for their siblings (or parents) at Christmas time and how those feelings have endured to the present.

Since some semblance of the saint is here to stay, we as a culture need to get the message of "creative deprivation" across to our offspring as well as to ourselves. For tucked away in the fabric of our own dreams is often the fantasy that some sort of savior-santa will someday deliver the perfect gift that he forgot to bring earlier in our lives.

On December 26th go to the stores and see how many disappointed people haven't been touched by love, faith, and hope—the truly sustaining gifts of life—but remain trapped in the clutches of greed. These frantic shoppers feel that if they can only just exchange their gifts for the right size and color or object, Christmas can be salvaged.

Colman McCarthy of the Washington Post sagely reminds us:

> We need to inform our family that life is often defined by limits, not only that we can't have everything but also that we can't and won't give everything. This is a hard notion in a country where nothing is off limits and all limits are off.

Another observation about Santa Claus. We've been looking for his gifts in the wrong place. We've been paying homage to him in shopping malls rather than in our own living rooms. We've been saluting his wares beyond our hearths rather than within our hearts.

Westerners who've grown out of the Judeo-Christian heritage should know better. As the spiritual descendants of the Bishop of Myra, we're invited to carry on his remarkably sobering yet relevant message, indeed ministry, in ways befitting our contemporary age. The commercial world has only as much power as we grant it. Santa Claus will always do as we are. No more and no less.

I'm not naive enough to think that we can dump the commercialized Santa Claus altogether. And I'm certainly not urging us to morph into Scrooges. I'm only recommending a conversion with respect to the manner in which we handle St. Nicholas. It would do his memory a greater justice and bring our world the enduring gifts for which it truly hungers.

If we're going to pass on the mythology of Santa Claus, let's embody the compassionate rather than commercialized version, the viable exemplar rather than a magical savior. Let's regale our children with some of the life-enhancing episodes of St. Nicholas. More specifically, let's show our offspring what it might mean to be disciples of this generous Advent saint.

I was singing last holiday season at a nursing home, one of my cherished weekly rituals. I croon in nursing homes, because it brings deep joy to all parties involved, myself included. One of the residents is a woman who goes by the self-created moniker of Jenifer Whisper. Jenifer happened to mention that her favorite carol as a child was *Jolly Old Saint Nicholas*. When I asked her why, she replied: "Because he bent his head low" to me, as a young girl, when others in the house couldn't be bothered to listen. "St. Nick became my buddy; we whispered to one another. St. Nick was someone I could count on to hear me and care about me!" Yes, early on in her life, Jenifer Whisper was fortunately blessed by the real Santa Claus!

St. Nicholas, through his great deeds, as the many legends show us, taught us exactly how to give, in secret, with no thought of any recompense. If we begin to emulate the wisdom of St. Nick's real ways, if we adults begin to give sometimes without knowledge and remuneration, our children will surely learn to follow suit. Wouldn't it be marvelous if, when our children stop believing in Santa Claus, they then actually morphed into Santas themselves? Wouldn't it be something if the little ones of the world were emboldened to "Santa Claus" someone at home, school, and in the larger world every day of their lives?

Following his example, I can envision family members sneaking around being "little Nicholases." A breakfast table is secretly set; a child's handwriting says, "This table was set for you by St. Nicholas." A pair of shoes is polished and snuck back into place. The family car is waxed and polished. A coat button is mysteriously sewn on again. We even slink around the neighborhood doing good for one another without seeking discovery or thanks.

We announce to the world: "I'm going to Santa Claus you" in the next month, and then we go about doing just that. And guess what? It might become habit-forming, and then the December spirit of generosity and graciousness mushrooms contagiously throughout the year and in every land.

Skimpy as the historical data may be, the odd twist is that Santa Claus was a real human being. He doesn't really resemble the "fat handshaking" character at department stores or some guy trying to navigate your chimney. He wasn't a "pretend person" like Peter Rabbit or Goldilocks, so we don't need to fantasize or fabricate him. He was a Bishop who gave gifts to the needy not the greedy. It isn't that we pay undue homage to Santa Claus. It's just to the wrong guy. The Bishop of Myra, the true source of the Santa Claus legends, if given a chance, could yet prove to be an effective, social fixture, a meaningful spiritual contributor, maybe even the semblance of some relevant worldwide hope.

Snowy Silence

"Silence is audible to all, at all times,
and in all places."
—HENRY DAVID THOREAU

The first snow day in the Midwest, there are normally hundreds of minor and major accidents. No matter how skilled and seasoned a motorist you are, sliding—even smashing into—others cars sometimes can't be avoided.

Back in the December of 1974, our first Christmas season living in Davenport, Iowa, I noticed Board meeting attendees leaving early, for seemingly inexplicable reasons. Well, they knew something I didn't. On this wintry night, beautiful, light snow flakes were accumulating into a full-out blizzard, and my spiritual cohorts were scurrying home. The last Board member finally called a halt to the meeting, so that whoever remained might drive home as swiftly and safely as possible.

So Carolyn and I exited the meeting, but we didn't make it home safely that night. Our new Pacer slid into some gulley on the outskirts of Bettendorf, a couple miles from our destination. Since this was before cell phones, our children were worried sick about what had happened to their parents. Fortunately, we were able to hoof it the distance home. But I didn't go to work that next day, and our West Coast brood was abruptly introduced to the first of many Midwestern snow days to follow.

That same Pacer was seemingly fated. On another cold and icy occasion, I was driving the hour-long trek across Interstate-80 from Davenport to Iowa City, to participate in a conference, when I suddenly skidded on undetected black ice, gliding off the highway into a massive ditch. Thankfully uninjured, I could only crawl across the snow-laden, frozen road to a nearby gas station to get help. While I was safe, the Pacer was wrecked for good; in retrospect, this was a blessing of sorts, since neither Carolyn nor I held much fondness for that particular model of car. To be sure, my hazardous, driving escapades in the snowy lands are relatively few and minor compared to veterans of the snow, but they're still mine, furnishing me with vivid and scary wake-up calls.

Nevertheless, while snow can be dangerous, it can also be deafening, creating a world of awe-inspiring mellowness. I never revisit my infrequent forays into the hoary hinterlands of the East and Midwest without recognizing, yea celebrating, its palpable serenity. Snow and silence are irrevocably yoked in my soul and evoke the passage from the Hebrew Scriptures: "the sound of a gentle stillness..." (I Kings 19:12).

Thirty years later, in the winter of 2004, I returned to the Midwest, this time to serve an interimship for six months in the resplendent and tranquil burg of Grand Rapids, Michigan. Many a day and night I would walk to and fro to my pastoral post, a mere two miles away. Rain, sleet, or sun, I rarely drove. Driving was too laborious, sometimes even tricky, plus it wasn't one iota as peaceful or picturesque. Sauntering to work beat motoring every time. The power of walking, albeit carefully, on slippery, snow-saturated sidewalks was absolutely spell-binding and memorable, still ingrained in the mind's eye and body's feel of this 5th generation Californian.

It was a particularly tender and nostalgic time for me in Grand Rapids. My beloved mother had just died, and I sought solitude to heal. Carolyn and I agreed that it would be wise for me to spend time apart and alone, on foreign turf, comforting myself even as I comforted others as the senior pastor at the renowned Fountain Street Church.

Although Carolyn flew back to companion me a few days after Christmas, I spent the bulk of the holiday season as a solitary pilgrim strolling the streets of this exquisite old Midwestern town. The lighted windows, frosted trees, and eerily silent, snow-soaked streets provided me with a Christmas experience different than any I had experienced before or ever since.

After preaching on Sunday morning, I would often practice a self-styled discipline of mindfulness by sauntering the streets of Grand Rapids from early evening into the night. It reminded me of the mystical tradition, where it's written: "Before the Word, there was silence." Before creation, before proclamation, and before chaos…there is silence.

As the transcendentalist Henry David Thoreau

penned: "Silence is audible to all, at all times, and in all places." In the presence of exquisite art, the stillness of an unstirring forest, the solemnity of majestic mountains, the peacefulness of gently falling snow, the ocean when waves are resting, amidst the ineffable wonder of human love or even in the face of unspeakable tragedy...in the presence of all these and much more, silence is audible. It resounds.

Stille Nacht

"Silent night! Holy night! All is calm all is bright
Round yon virgin mother and child
Holy infant so tender and mild
Sleep in heavenly peace! Sleep in heavenly peace!"
—JOHN FREEMAN YOUNG (ENGLISH TRANSLATION)

The following story is variously reported, but what follows is roughly the narrative with which I'm most familiar.

It was Christmas Eve in a little mountain village in Austria. The village priest was preparing the Christmas message. However, he was called out to baptize a child born in the bitter cold. Despite the emergency interruption, the priest found himself strangely moved by the mother and child. A hope for the future had been generated by this singular birth. Stirred by the stars blanketing a black sky, the pastor trod back to the church where the annual service was to be conducted, and deep in his heart he had now truly come to comprehend the miracle of birth. He began to compose a poem that was soon laid aside.

Then two years later, the unexpected happened again. On Christmas Eve, 1818, the organ of St. Nicholas Church, Oberndorf, Bavaria, was in dire need of repair, since a mouse, as mice are wont to do, had been hunting for something upon which to gnaw. The mouse found it and immediately started to nibble on the church organ, chewing its way through the straps that held the bellows.

An immediate crisis arose. How could this congregation celebrate the important Christmas Eve service without their organ? Franz Gruber, the church organist, presented the predicament to Joseph Mohr, the vicar of the church, urging that some form of music was essential to animate the souls of parishioners.

Fortunately, the priest remembered the poem he'd composed. Mohr took the verse and ran to the local schoolmaster who happened to play the guitar. In the hours before the service, the two worked feverishly against the deadline. As time drew nigh, congregants desolately filed into the silent church. Their spirits were immediately heartened, as the priest and the schoolmaster together caroled the brand new song to the chords of the guitar. "Stille nacht, heilige nacht," they sang. The plainness of lyrics combined with the soothing beauty of music brought the gathered congregants to tears of gratitude and joy.

Whenever this exquisite carol (translated into more than 90 different languages and dialects) is sung, with or without accompaniment of guitar or organ, it rekindles for most of us precious childhood memories of lighted Christmas trees and candles in darkened houses of worship or homes of solace and succor.

For me, singing *Stille Nacht* accounts for two of my most unforgettable Christmas Eve worship services: first, singing it in a parish in West Berlin, Germany in 1968, where I served as Assistant Pastor; and, second, when my friend John and I sang *Stille Nacht*, again in its original German, strumming our own guitars in tandem back in 1999. When everyone joined us, first in German, then in Spanish, and finally in English... chills ran down my spine and flooded my soul.

Arriving on Epiphany Sunday

"Christmas, my child, is love in action.
Every time we love,
every time we give,
it's Christmas."
—DALE EVANS

We had just been married a month, when, the day after Christmas, Carolyn and I with 3 of our 4 children (ages 5-12) headed eastward from sunny California to snowy Iowa, in two beat-up cars, affectionately named the *Blue Beetle* (Datsun) and the *Green Grasshopper* (Volkswagen). We were leaving parents and other family as well as generational California rootage and heading straightway into the wintry blasts of the Midwest. None of our children had spent any time in snow. Carolyn, who had lived in California and Hawaii for all her days, was in for a shocking treat as well. I, the only snow-veteran in our newly-formed clan, possessed but limited familiarity with frost and blizzards, going to college in Pennsylvania, the first time I'd ever left the state of California. Little did we know that late December of 1973 would provide some of the fiercest storms of the century, all across America.

As the wise men arrived at the Bethlehem birth on January 6th, Epiphany Sunday, so we entered the Quad Cities on that very auspicious Sunday, centuries later. What follows are excerpts (slightly modified) from my first sermon delivered to our Davenport, Iowa congregation, composed while sitting in the *Daryl Motors, Inc.* garage in Des Moines, Iowa, having both cars overhauled, readying our exhausted and weather-beaten family for the final three hour push into the Quad Cities. Actually, we had to return, two days later, to pick up the *Green Grasshopper*, which was too hobbled to complete the stretch on schedule.

Understandably, this 1974 homily, written on the actual stationery of an auto shop, has become something of a family heirloom.

My dear, new Quad Cities congregants:

Our 2000 mile holiday jaunt across our beloved land has truly been a tragicomedy. It's impossible to recapitulate the highs and lows of our journey, but I'd like to relate a few tales, since they're so fresh on our hearts. I promise you that next week, I'll get back to preaching on more "normal" religious themes. I ask you to bear with me as we bare our souls a bit.

Let me say, it was a good, solid coalescing time for us as a brand new family. The kids were relatively good, we parents were relatively good...altogether, we were relatively good as we migrated East. I think you understand my "drift," which is surely the right word to use, given our jaunt through blizzard after blizzard.

The main problem has been our cars, especially my VW, the Green Grasshopper, born in Germany but having lived its entire 6 ½ year life only in sunny California. It started swearing and conking out about Kansas. No actually earlier than that.

We were just outside Birdwater, New Mexico (honest that was the name of the town) when one of our jalopies, which is what they are, the Blue Beetle (Carolyn's Datsun) started smoking up a storm. Wouldn't you know it, the Beetle stalled on the Interstate Saturday and Sunday, New Year's Eve and New Year's Day respectively. Great times to seek emergency roadside assistance, right?

With Carolyn steering, the 3 kids (remember they didn't ask to sign up for this new family arrangement, trekking blindly to a faraway land!) and I pushed the car off the freeway; then we were fortunately towed into a nearby gas station. That was tow #1. The weather was freezing by now, on its way down, down, down in temperature and wind chill, familiar realities to you Midwesterners but foreign to our California bodies!

A couple days later, our five-year-old son Rusty got his hand caught in the car door amidst an ice storm. He was yelping as we took him to a nearby hospital. Luckily, he had no fractures. At least, something wasn't broken! But it seemed like even the car door was against us, since this crisis happened in Liberal, Kansas. Didn't this town know who we were, progressives and all that?

Then there was a night of relief and delight, as we stayed with my brother's family in Topeka, Kansas. I remember the kids having a blast racing around in Phil's snowmobiles which functioned more smoothly and puttered more swiftly than either of our banged-up, ill-prepared cars.

We left the warmth and affection of my brother's abode, headed east, then the next day, one of our cars wouldn't start, and there was no one around to tow us for hours. Then tow #2 miraculously occurred. Everything was balanced, tuned, and timed in our two cars for the final entry into our new Midwestern home.

Alas, on the turnpike just outside Des Moines the gas line of the Grasshopper froze up, and the Beetle had to push brother Grasshopper, along with assistance from four of us again, off the highway. Tow #3: this time into a garage in Des Moines, where our car happily stored in the shop while we all slept in a nearby hotel that seemed considerably colder and more dilapidated than the garage. But after all they'd been through, our cars deserved a reasonable night's sleep, okay? We would get ours later, a few days later...or would it be weeks?

My sermon continues:

Okay, my new congregation of strangers, soon to be spiritual companions, we're not asking on Epiphany Sunday for sympathy so much as a chance to vent our cross-country saga, get it out of our systems, so with patience from all of us, we can in due course integrate ourselves into the beauty of Iowa's heartland as well as into each of your own hearts. You've already been incredibly gracious and hospitable to the Chapman-Towle clan. Thank you, thank you, thank you.

The five of us are currently way off the Rahe psycho-social stress chart: what with being in a new land, new marriage, new family constellation, new church community, new job, and a new home.

But have no fear, just as the wise men have arrived, bearing gifts, we come bearing our own, as well as eager and ready to receive your offerings. I feel good and sufficiently solid within myself and with all the chosen matches of my life now.

Notice I said "sufficiently solid!"

The story of your Unitarian church in Daven-
port, Iowa—having launched in 1868—is far
older than the ages of our family totaled together.
You came before us and will endure long after
us. We will share but an interval together. How-
ever, my fervent hope is that during our shared
ministry we will be daring and compassionate,
boldly exploring our own peculiar blend of joy
and sorrow and caring as we each dance to our
own drummers during this sacred spell together.

I am a pastor of, by, and for the people; that's
simply how I do ministry. So our congregational
life will be run democratically and open-hearted-
ly. I assure you, we share the ministry of this be-
loved community. It's not mine; it's not yours; it
*will be **ours**! May we share it wisely, fairly, and*
respectfully. May we become a truly intergen-
erational community where there is an enrich-
ing ministry to youth, adult, and child alike...
within and beyond the walls of this historic site
on the hill.

So, as we arrive here in the pulpit on Epiphany
Sunday, the Wise Men are also just getting into
town for a new birth, bringing sacks of gold,

myrrh, and frankincense. They came from the East, whereas we arrive from the West. They were the first religious figures to worship Jesus. Well, this Chapman-Towle clan of five constitute religious figures too, but only in the same way that you and you and you are equally religious figures.

We too have come to worship Jesus; well, I'd rather say that we've come to worship the values and visions of the man Jesus as well as the count-less other exemplary spiritual and prophetic sis-ters and brothers found in the numerous stables of human history.

I want to close with words of Paul who wrote to the church in Corinth: "Faith, hope, and love abide, but the greatest of these is love." Well, probably love is the greatest, yet faith, hope, and love will all be critical nurturants in our budding church family. If the gifts of the magi were gold, myrrh, and frankincense, ours will not be mate-rial but *spiritual gifts, they will be faith, hope, and love...gifts we bring to each other, gifts we must share together, if our ministerial marriage is to flourish and touch myriad lives far, far, far into seasons beyond our counting...*
So, I summon us to honor faith, hope, and love

on this Epiphany Sunday and in the days and nights ahead.

Let us keep the faith, let us offer the hope, and let us share the love...and when we aren't always able to keep the faith or able to offer much hope, let's never forget, at least, to share enough love, one with another. Yes, enough love is what we all need!

After the sermon, I sat down, only to realize that our five-year-old son Rusty had, earlier in the service, left our family seated in the front row of the church and had mounted the dais, unobtrusively taking his own seat in the chancel chair across from me. When I asked Rusty why? Our little boy calmly and clearly answered: "Well, this church is my place too. It belongs to me too!" So it did, and so it still does...

When we belong to a religious community and it belongs to us, the gathered congregation becomes, both literally and mystically, beloved. And within the embrace of such a beloved community, we're able to welcome the joy and sadness, service and silence inherent in life's major celebrations...including Christmas itself.

My prayerful hope for everyone is that each and every Christmas—whether we experience it in the West or East, South or North or in the Midwest—

might become a full-souled celebration rather than a compulsory annual tour of duty. Or as brother Dickens would insist:

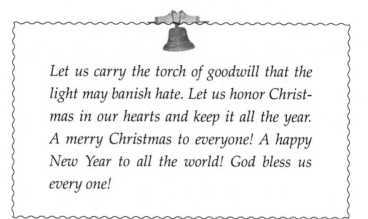

Let us carry the torch of goodwill that the light may banish hate. Let us honor Christmas in our hearts and keep it all the year. A merry Christmas to everyone! A happy New Year to all the world! God bless us every one!

About Tom Owen-Towle

The Rev. Dr. Tom Owen-Towle has been a parish minister since 1967 and is the author of two dozen books on personal relationships and spiritual growth.

Tom and his life-partner, the Rev. Dr. Carolyn Sheets Owen-Towle, are the active parents of four children and seven grandchildren. Tom is a guitarist, parlor magician, tennis player, and currently sings with seniors, mentors children and youth, and volunteers with San Diego's homeless.

Owen-Towle is a national leader who continues to conduct workshops and retreats on the core themes of his books.

For more information about Tom Owen-Towle's writings, visit: www.tomo-t.com

Made in the USA
Lexington, KY
16 July 2017